HACKNEY
Memories

ALAN WILSON

SUTTON PUBLISHING

Sutton Publishing Limited
Phoenix Mill · Thrupp · Stroud
Gloucestershire · GL5 2BU

First published 2004

Copyright © Alan D. Wilson, 2004

Frontispiece: The author in 1938, aged ten.
(Author's collection)

British Library Cataloguing in Publication Data
A catalogue record for this book is available from the
British Library.

ISBN 0-7509-3716-5

Typeset in 10.5/13.5 Photina.
Typesetting and origination by
Sutton Publishing Limited.
Printed and bound in England by
J.H. Haynes & Co. Ltd, Sparkford.

In memory of my parents Thomas Arthur Wilson
and Louisa Harriet Wilson (née Pruden)
who gave me a happy childhood

CONTENTS

ACKNOWLEDGEMENTS

I am indebted to Tom Lee of the Paddle Steamer Picture Gallery for his enthusiastic help and supply of pictures of paddle steamers and motor vessels and allowing them to be used, and to St Luke's Church, Hackney, for giving me the photograph of the Church Hall.

I would like to thank the following organisations for permission to publish illustrations from their collections and for the help of their staff: the Hackney Archives Department of the Borough of Hackney, David Mander, Borough Archivist and Peter Kent; the London Metropolitan Archives (LMA) and Rhys Griffith, Principal Archivist; the Trustees of the Imperial War Museum (IWM); the estate of C.R.W. Nevington/Bridgeman Art Library and the Radio Times Magazine; the Hulton-Getty Picture Library

I also wish to acknowledge the skills and guidance of Simon Fletcher and Matthew Brown of Sutton Publishing.

Lastly, I thank my wife, Margaret Wilson, for her punctilious reading of the manuscript, perceptive comments and constant support, not to mention her general patience. I also thank Mary Barker for reading the manuscript so carefully. I remember, too, my mother who over the long years assiduously kept and guarded many of the photographs and memorabilia reproduced in this book.

Alan Wilson
Liphook
March 2004

1 A Silver-Plated Spoon

I was born in 1928, when peace was at its zenith and the British Empire splashed red across the globe; never had it reached a greater extent and never had it appeared more powerful. It was an empire on which the sun never set, although James Joyce said that this was because God did not trust the English. But, sceptics apart, the sun of Empire shone brightly on all, and the sky seemed cloudless. Alas, before long that sun was to set and there would follow a sinister twilight of troubled peace and the darkness of prolonged war. The Empire and its greatness were soon to go, but we did not know that then, for none but the wise knew that the glittering imperial robe was but the shroud of a corpse. The majority, whether they stood in frock-coats or rags, were still proud of the Empire.

English cricket was at its height. Jack Hobbs still batted gracefully at the Oval, while the mighty Hammond effortlessly stroked the ball high over cover. Larwood, Tate and J.C. White skittled their opponents out, and in the fullness of their pride English bowlers had no need of body-line. Bradman's time had yet to come. English tennis, too, was about to revive with the young Perry although, for the moment, the four French musketeers ruled the tennis world while Big Bill Tilden glowered across the Atlantic from his fastness in Forest Hills. Glasses still jingled in the speakeasies of America and Al Capone ruled openly over his gangster empire in the Loop. The aged Hindenburg reigned over a quiescent Germany and, for the moment, Hitler was in decline. Coolidge presided serenely in the White House; the financial collapse of Wall Street, and its portentous consequences, were yet to come. Peace was at its height.

I was born into this world on the first day of spring, 21 March. I had been due on 1 April, an expectation that was a source of considerable worry to my mother – indeed, it appears that this was her principal concern. But, fortunately for her peace of mind, I was in a hurry to meet the world – don't ask me why – and was born ten days early, thus avoiding the mistake of arriving on a day dedicated to the follies of mankind. I much prefer my spring day.

My birthplace was in the East End of London at the home of my mother's parents, 13 Beale Place, just off the Roman Road; a lively, living place. As I grew up I became very familiar with this house where the greater family gathered. Each week without fail all the married daughters and their husbands paid a visit to Nan and Grandad. This was before the universal motor car and the weekend outing. But the greater family died with the war, as did the house. No. 13 does not exist now, nor does the rest of Beale Place for that matter. All the houses were blown to pieces by Adolf Hitler. There is not a brick left, nor, indeed, so much as a mark on the London street map, for the area was redeveloped after the war. Beale Place was literally wiped off the map, and with it part of me.

My mother was a slight, talkative woman with a quicksilver tongue. I am sure she would have made a fine advocate given the chance and as a child I could never tell a lie without being exposed by her forensic skills. I found it simpler to tell the truth. Mother was born a minute baby – Nan said she could have been put in a pint pot – and the doctor did not expect her to live. In this the doctor was mistaken by some eighty-seven years. Father always thought that Mother was a scatterbrain. Maybe she was, but she had a native, if untrained, intelligence and a quick wit. She was difficult to defeat in argument as she had a patented, perverse and persistent logic of her own.

My father, like myself, was a large man, over 6 foot tall; in this he took after his father. He was sensitive, hot-tempered, but intensely loyal. To this day I remember his hands were large but gentle and his fingers were like bananas. But they were skilful: he was a good amateur cabinet-maker.

For the first two years of my life I lived in Cadogan Terrace, on the second floor of a flat that overlooked Victoria Park. The park played an important part in my early life and is my first memory. I was lying in a large old-fashioned pram pushed by my mother along a pavement that skirted the park when my eyes took in a view of a strange flickering world of grass and trees; it was like a scene from an old silent film. I was looking through a passing fence of chestnut palings. Its oddity impressed itself on my memory and remains with me to this day. I was less than one year old.

Later I remember toddling in the landlord's cabbage patch at the rear of the house and looking in wonderment at steam trains that rumbled by on the railway track at the end of the garden, puffing out white clouds interlaced with streamers of black soot. For this was the age of steam, and steam never fails to excite both young and old.

But strange are the ways of memory. For although I remember these inconsequential events, I do not have the slightest recollection of my tryst with death during the Christmas of 1928. I was just nine months old and had contracted pneumonia. And I have no recall at all of my fight for life, nor of the closeness of the struggle, for there were no antibiotics then. Strange that one remembers trivialities while forgetting the dramas of life.

My mother was certain that I had picked up the infection at a baby show. If this is so, then I still have a permanent reminder of that event and its dramatic sequel. I came second, a result that rankled with my mother –

In readiness for a baby competition. I came second and won the silver-plated spoon shown. I also caught pneumonia and nearly died. (*Author's collection*)

she had expectations that were altogether too great. Most of us are the also-rans of life – that is, if you look on life as a race. But there was a consolation prize for this failure. I had not been born with a silver spoon in my mouth – nothing so uncomfortable – but I acquired a silver spoon that day, for that was the second prize. It had a teddy bear handle and I have treasured it to this day. But I have to confess that it was only silver on the surface. Below was nickel and copper.

My struggle with pneumonia took the traditional course in those days before antibiotics. My temperature rose to 104°F and stayed there for days. Our doctor warned my parents that a 'crisis' would come when nature would make the decision: life or death. The crisis did come and my temperature plummeted. In an hour it was below normal, but my heartbeat dropped with it. My mother called the doctor. 'Should I give him brandy, doctor?' 'I have something better, Mrs Wilson. Strychnine.' It worked and I lived to see my first Christmas.

There was another crisis – a financial one. My parents had exhausted their meagre savings. There was little left, but the doctor still continued to call, unasked for. Unlike today, doctors were assiduous with their house calls. Was it because before the National Health Service there was an extra fee for call-out? Whatever the reason, the frequent house calls of the doctor became a cause of great concern to my parents. Their savings, so slowly accumulated over the long years, had gone and there was a stark choice between doctor's fees and the necessities of life – food and rent.

My parents were desperate to do their best for me. Not to have the doctor when he was needed lay on their conscience. Granny Wilson was asked to give of her sound practical wisdom. She was certain and blunt. 'He doesn't need the doctor any more. The doctor's only coming for the money.' Mother was embarrassed, for the doctor had saved my life. 'I'll do it,' said Granny, and so she did. Today, telling a doctor not to call seems very strange.

I have no other memories of those early days except the mantelpiece. It was just an ordinary mantelpiece of dark oak, but in my infant mind it was the symbol of home. The fire in the hearth lies deep in the human psyche, deeper, by far, I think, than the television set. And it was to be the first lost thing of my life. For the time was to come when my parents decided that the flat was too small and we would have to leave. We went to 12 Darnley Road. I remember standing in the living room of the new home staring desolately at a white marble mantelpiece. In my distress I cried out: 'I want my old mantelpiece! I want my old mantelpiece!' And burst into bitter tears.

2   Home – 12 Darnley Road

We left Cadogan Terrace to live in a tree-lined street, Darnley Road, which lies just off busy Mare Street, the artery of Hackney. It was a quiet road where the wealthy and the poor, workers and professionals, Jew and Gentile, lived side by side.

Our home was 12 Darnley Road, a stately Victorian four-storey terraced house with a flight of balustraded stone steps that led to an elevated ground floor. Inside the main entrance was an old-fashioned, spacious entrance hall, well lit by the coloured light that filtered through the stained-glass windows of the front door. On this floor were the sitting-room, dining-room and study. Above were two more floors with bedrooms. The bathroom, an afterthought, was on a mezzanine floor. Of course, we did not live in this part of the house; no, this was the domain of the middle-class Hubbles; we lived down in the basement or, as Father insisted on saying, semi-basement. He said this with some pride, making the best of a bad job, ever the dreamer. In truth, as Mother, ever the realist, said, it was a sunless place.

My first memories of the house are of my mother struggling up the 'airy' (basement area) steps with a small collapsible pushchair, and me. I did not like that pushchair, for it was much less comfortable than my full-sized baby pram. Nevertheless, it was better than walking. Sadly the day came when my mother left the pushchair behind in the passageway. I looked around puzzled. 'You can walk today,' she told me. This I did not like; indeed I felt hurt and deprived. I am inclined physically to be indolent and no doubt this characteristic showed up at a very early stage in life.

In our basement home the kitchen was my favourite room; it was full of interest. It was not one of those fitted kitchens of today's gleaming white or bogus oak. It was the ultimate in an unfitted kitchen. The kitchen had a dresser, a deal table, an easywork made from a piece of office furniture, and a motley collection of chairs. There was an old gas stove, with a maze of exposed pipes, and a butler sink with brass taps. Everything happened in the kitchen. There we ate, there we washed up, there I had my weekly bath and there my mother did the weekly wash. The weekly wash was done with equipment that is now only to be found in museums: the zinc washtub, the wooden dolly, the scrubbing board and large mangle with wooden rollers. Life was hard work in those days.

There was an old-fashioned fireplace: one of those huge Victorian grates, a tall black basket with half a dozen cast-iron bars. Such things have long been swept away by the dictates of fashion and comfort. Even in the thirties they were becoming unfashionable and a sure sign of being poor and behind the times. People were just beginning to aspire to fashionable things, and tiled fireplaces were becoming popular for those who could afford them. Nowadays the Victorian grates are once more appreciated and much sought-after.

This fireplace fascinated me. Often it was dead and filled with screwed-up newspaper to catch the soot that fell down the chimney. But just once in a while, on a cold winter's day, the fire was lit and then it would consume coals like Satan's furnace and glow like a great basket of red and black coals and white ash. A fierce heat radiated from this pyre that seared face and arms; it also sucked in cold streams of air from every crack and crevice, so one was at once roasted and chilled. But if open fires were not as comfortable as central heating, they were infinitely more interesting than flat radiators.

Mother told me to look for faces in the fire. And sure enough they were there when I gazed at the red-hot coals and the yellow flames that writhed between them. I saw the fiery demons of the fire come and go, grotesque peoples of the flames, their faces of red and black breathing out yellow smoke, ever-changing in shape and size, transient creatures that existed for the moment before crumbling in the flames. This fiery dance of the ephemerals fascinated me for hours. So it was that I loved those winter days, in that time before computers when children had to use their imagination and find their own amusements.

Bath night in Darnley Road in the 1930s was an arduous affair, but not lacking in interest. It was not a routine daily occurrence but an exciting, and for me a dreaded, weekly event. My bath was taken in the kitchen before a red roaring fire. It was a family affair. First, Father placed a great zinc bath on the floor and dismay crept in my heart. In vain I protested, 'Dad! I've kept clean this week!' He and Mother laughed. 'I don't need a bath!' But my pleas were ignored. Kettles and saucepans were filled to the brim with water and put on the gas stove. Soon clouds of steam filled the kitchen. The moment of truth was at hand.

Father emptied the kettles and pans into the zinc bath. Steam billowed, only to be quenched by buckets of cold water. Meanwhile, Mother undressed me and my morale plummeted. I stood naked, scorched on one side by the fire and frozen on the other by cold draughts. Then came the dreaded plunge into the water. Gradually I relaxed but not for long, for soon mother was lathering me all over with a hard bar of Sunlight soap. It was not pleasant, as her hands were rough. 'Mum, you're hurting! Let Dad do it!' So Dad would take over with his large but gentle big hands. They were almost too gentle for they sensitised my skin and raised goose pimples.

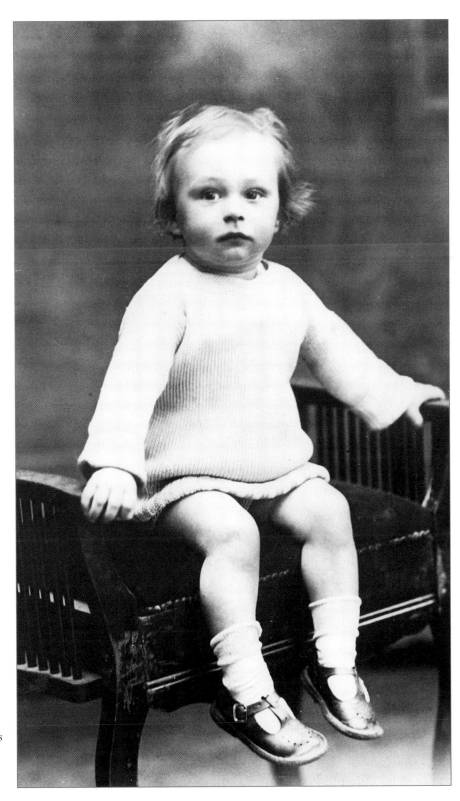

A posed photograph, 1931, a torture that I was put through on occasions.
(Author's collection)

Covered with soap, I waited for the worst moment. It came with the pouring of a jug of water over my head. It was either too hot or too cold. Water flooded my face, into my eyes and ears. I held my breath and clenched my teeth. Then I had to stand up, face the heat and the chill, and be dried. Dad said, with a broad smile, 'That wasn't too bad, son, was it?' I didn't agree. Bath night was not my favourite night. As I dressed, mother and father undertook the tedious process of emptying the bath with bucket and saucepan. The zinc bath would be taken out and hung on an airy wall.

When I was older Mrs Hubble offered the use of her bathroom on the mezzanine floor. There was an old-fashioned enamelled bath that rested on four ornamental legs and above it a ferocious geyser of glowing brass that consumed pennies and ejected scalding hot water. Geyser was an apt description. On ignition, there was a terrifying rocket-like whoosh followed by a moment of fear as boiling water gushed forth in turbulent flow. Such were the thrills of taking baths in those days!

One bath night I formed a cunning plan and persuaded my parents to let me bath myself. 'I'm getting a big boy now!' My idea was to mimic bathing without the unpleasant experience of immersion. So I splashed away with one hand in the bath water for some minutes. But my performance was not convincing. My parents burst in and caught me in my deception. I was surprised when they laughed and did not get angry. I have always found it very difficult to get away with anything.

When I look back from the perspective of the early twenty-first century, I realise that our household was remarkably free of gadgets. For the poor, and many of the rich, household technology was little different from Victorian days. There was no washing machine. Washing was done in a tub and clothes cleaned with bar soap on a scrubbing board. There was no electric iron. The irons my mother used were heavy cast-iron objects; they are prized antiques today. They were heated by the coal fire in winter or on the gas stove in summer. There was no vacuum cleaner, although middle-class Mrs Hubble upstairs had an ancient Hoover. The broom and duster, supplemented by a battered Ewbank carpet-sweeper, had to suffice for cleaning. The air was always dusty. But I liked dust and watched its haphazard flight in our dark rooms where it sparkled in slivers of light.

There was no refrigerator, so our food was stored outside in the cool airy, in a meat safe. The only kitchen appliance was the mincer. We did not have a telephone. What on earth would you do with a telephone when your relations were so near?

Needless to say, we did not have a motor car, nor did we ever think of having one. We could not afford one. We did not need one. Our weekend outings were not to the seaside but to my grandparents who lived within easy walking distance. That was fun enough. Rarely did we stray beyond the confines of our family area. Even the Hubbles did not have a car and they *could* afford one. The truth is that in those days cars were not ingrained in the culture as they are today. They were not an essential element of transport. One of the Hubble sons had one, but it was a sporty affair for fun and not utility.

The electric bell I remember with affection, for it had an antediluvian charm. It was powered by an old-fashioned wet battery, a Leclanché cell, a square 2-pint jar containing a liquid in which was immersed a zinc and carbon rod. Unlike the modern dry battery, you could see how it worked. It also lasted for ever.

There was a home-made wireless of my father's. I say wireless as 'radio' seems a too-sophisticated term to apply to that contraption; if anything it reminded me of a miniature version of Osterley Park. It had two towers, one at each end of a broad façade. The towers were my father's idea of concealing the lead accumulators. Inside the main housing were four stout thermionic valves, their filaments glowing red from the power provided by the accumulators. A high-tension battery (HT) of 140 volts activated the receiver and amplifier. A separate horn loudspeaker completed the assemblage. The thermionic valve and the horn speaker have passed into technological limbo, as have the HT battery and wet accumulators – for this we must be thankful. Today we buy wonderful miniaturised sets or sophisticated hi-fis that work like a dream, but somehow they lack the simple fun of those early receivers.

For years this pioneering construction of my father's hung around 12 Darnley Road waiting for him to do something about it. I would constantly ask the irritating questions: 'Why doesn't it work, Daddy?' or 'Why don't you get it to work, Daddy?' The problem was that the HT batteries were expensive, consisting of eighty or so cells linked in series, and the lead accumulators that fed the greedy thermionic valves ran down rapidly. These heavy and messy objects filled with sulphuric acid had to be carted to an electrical shop for recharging once a week. Not surprisingly, our wireless set normally operated with exhausted batteries and accumulators.

My father, like others, tried to prolong the life of the HT batteries by baking them in the oven. In the end he gave up, for it was too costly on his wage to keep the wireless going. I never remember hearing any programmes on my father's wireless set. We had to wait until 1937, when the all-mains Philco radio arrived, before we could listen to broadcasts regularly. But that is to miss the point; in those days the magic of wireless and the reception of the faint invisible signals was enough; its content mattered not.

For home entertainment there was a piano, rarely played, and a portable wind-up gramophone. The gramophone was more important than the wireless. It was to the modern compact disc player what a chariot is to the Rolls-Royce. In place of the glistening CD and delicate laser beam were the old 78rpm shellac records that shattered if dropped, and brutal steel needles. There was no electronic amplifier, only a 'sound box' and a trumpet loudspeaker. The machine was tedious to use for it had to be wound up for every record and each record only lasted 3 minutes. Nevertheless I enjoyed the gramophone and listened endlessly to the strains of 'Colonel Bogey', 'In a Monastery Garden' and 'In a Persian Market'. What has happened to those popular tunes today? Another favourite of mine was 'Nigger Minstrels', presided over by a Mr Interlocutor, who was constantly harassed by one Mr Bones who played the bones.

Otherwise I played with my toys. None was plastic. There were tin soldiers: redcoats with muskets, Zulus with assegais and plumed officers prancing on horses, but there were no tanks. There was a Meccano set of grey metal which, although it gave much pleasure, was far too small for my grandiose plan to build a model of the Tower Bridge. Then there was a large brass Magic Lantern – those were the days before 35mm slide projectors – converted from oil to electricity and projecting a slide of the forlorn wreckage of the R101. But nearest to my heart was a large clockwork Hornby train set, alas to be lost to me forever with the advent of war.

Mr Hubble, our landlord and owner of the house, was a middle-class friend of father's; one of the business and professional classes who still lived in Hackney. He was a solidly built man with the grave, self-assured face of the wholesale grocer he was. To me as a child, the Hubbles were an awesome, cultured family, denizens of another world. We were divided from them by a flight of linoleum-clad stairs that led upward from our basement passageway to a green baize door, the entrance to that other world. Here the cold linoleum gave way to warm carpeting. I was forbidden to climb those stairs. The urbane world above was not for me. But once I did venture up them and penetrated into Mr Hubble's lush study lined with books: a whole room given over to learning. I took to it instantly and aspired to it.

That was 12 Darnley Road, also known as Tudor House, a happy place and the place of my childhood. Darnley Road is no more, at least the side on which no. 12 stood is no more since a land mine destroyed it. It now forms part of the playground of a school. Strangely, the other side of Darnley Road is unchanged, much as it was all those years ago. When I face that way, with my back to the playground, I can imagine that nothing has changed. Then I turn round. I see the asphalt plain that is on the other side, my side, the obliterated side of Darnley Road, and see that everything has changed. When I lay in my childhood bed staring at the ceiling I imagined many things, but I never dreamt that one day it would be turned into asphalt and children would play games where Mr Hubble had his study.

3 *Hackney*

The pre-war Hackney was not the Hackney of today. Old landmarks have been demolished and it lies under the shadows of the all-conquering tower blocks. But not all has changed. Hackney station and the railway viaduct over Mare Street are still to be seen, much as they were in the latter half of the nineteenth century.

Nearby are the remnants of an even older Hackney: the old Regency Town Hall, now a bank, and behind it the isolated tower of St Augustine's. The tower is all that remains of a medieval foundation. Further back is the 'new' parish church of St John's that replaced the old church in the eighteenth century. By the railway bridge is a dip in the road that marks the site of the old village pond, for Hackney was once a village. This pond or 'mere' is the 'mere' in Mare Street. The pond was formed by a ford of the long-lost Hackney Brook which once crossed Mare Street.

Further along Mare Street is the Hackney Empire, that cockney baroque fantasy with its bulbous towers owing something to Byzantium – one of the last Edwardian music halls in London. These towers of bygone ages – the Edwardian, the Regency and the Gothic – are the survivors of the Hackney that was. But although they survive, they no longer dominate.

The air is clearer now. Then, the skies were always murky and the days of my Hackney childhood were lived under a perpetual hazy canopy the colour of lentil soup. After a seaside holiday I wept when returning to Hackney and saw the dusky hues of its skies and its dull grey streets. I yearned for the bright colours of the seaside with its golden sands and deep blue sea.

The social scene of Hackney has changed. Before the war it was a warm place housing a mixed community: rich man, poor man, Jew and Gentile all coexisted humanely in two- or three-storey houses. Life then was not packaged in hygienic cellophane. Horses with their oat bags struggled and sweated under heavy loads on cobbled streets; the sweet smell of their sweat mingled with the odour of petrol fumes. Water troughs were still in place on all the main streets. Once, on a wet day, I saw a horse slip on a greasy road and collapse in a muddle between the shafts. An angry driver whipped the poor trapped animal as it tried to struggle on its feet. The cruelty of that scene stays vividly in my memory. In Well Street the occasional flock of sheep was to be seen as they were shepherded along

their way to a slaughterhouse. These things were reminders of a village past, when my grandmother could stand in Morning Lane and look across fields to Hackney Marsh. There was death as well as life in the Hackney of those days. In the butcher's, carcasses of animals hung in gory display blatantly proclaiming their origins.

There was a dark side to these picturesque scenes. There was the bluebottle and other members of the fly family who had a fancy both for horses' droppings and for foods that were exposed for sale in dairies and butcher's shops. Sooner or later we children fell ill with the fevers of the town. We would boast to each other of the diseases we had had. I was low in this pecking order, with but pneumonia, whooping cough, measles and diphtheria to my name. To my shame I missed out on scarlet fever, mumps and chickenpox. There were many fever hospitals to accommodate us, and more were being built as war broke out, but after the war they were not needed as fevers disappeared from London streets. Hygiene had improved and antibiotics had arrived.

Trams still rattled down Mare Street and dominated the street scene. There were no overhead wires; instead the trams picked up their current via a conduit that ran between the rails. It was Grandfather Wilson's humble job to clean these out at night. Once he had been an ostler in the days of the horse trams, but those days had gone and he was reduced to this. It never crossed my young mind that the day would come when these dinosaurs of transport would go. But go they would, for soon the trolleybus would arrive. These had first appeared in the seaside towns and Dickie Drage had boasted to me that he had ridden on one of these marvels of the

Hackney station, Mare Street, 1930. Trams were still in use in those days. After it ceased to be used as a station there were plans to close it, but it is now used as a market. A station reopened many years later but in a new building nearby. *(Hackney Archives)*

age when on holiday. I was suitably impressed by his adventure. Eventually they came to Hackney and excited our curiosity. We boys would ask each other: 'Have you had a ride on a trolleybus?' Our eyes were wide open as we gazed at what were little more than trams without tracks. Now our eyes are dulled by a surfeit of technological achievement.

Ancient double-decker buses vied with trams on the streets of Hackney. They carried history with them. The conductor still spoke of 'inside' instead of 'downstairs' and 'outside' instead of 'upstairs'. They were strange vehicles. At the rear was a curling open staircase apparently stuck on as an afterthought. It resembled a fire escape. Climbing that staircase on a wet and windy day was an unpleasant experience that still sticks in my memory. I did not know then that it told the story of the evolution of the London double-decker. Sometime in the previous century, in the days of the stagecoach, second-class passengers had been accommodated on the roof and the horse omnibus adopted this practice. A ladder had been added for the convenience of the passengers. This arrangement had survived the passing of the horse omnibus and was to be found in the early petrol buses,

Trams being directed by police at the Hackney Road–Cambridge Heath Road junction. *(LMA)*

where the upper deck was open, literally outside, and was only later roofed in. But the staircase was left, as it had been in the days of the stagecoach, open to the elements. At the end of the thirties the final step was taken and the staircase enclosed.

Shire horses pulled coal carts black with dust. On top of piled black sacks, coalmen stood clad in black aprons and strange black hoods, red eyes glittering strangely in their blackened faces. These apparitions were hawking coal and shouting out their prices: 'One and eleven' – 1s 11d per hundredweight. Great horses pulled brewers' drays that drew up outside public houses. I would watch the brewers' men roll wooden barrels down curious concave ladders on to the pavement and thence, via a manhole, into the cellars below.

There were also smaller horses that pulled a variety of carts; I remember the milk carts best. Through the mists of time they appear beautiful things, with bright churns bound by gleaming brass hoops. A ladle drooped by the churn and a smile adorned the face of a cheerful milkman who, more often than not, wore a striped apron. I once had to write an essay on why a horse was better than a motor-van for delivering milk. What did I say? That the horse was better at starting and stopping than the petrol engine.

A tram of the 1930s. (LMA)

Officials
questioning a man
delivering sacks of
coal from a horse-
drawn cart.
(LMA)

That while the milkman was delivering the milk a well-trained horse would move on to the next door.

Another horse-drawn vehicle was sometimes to be seen in Hackney – the funeral carriage. Funerals were different in those days. Black-plumed horses drawing black coaches were still to be seen, a stately entourage suitable for the dignity of a funeral. I was taught by my mother always to show respect. So when a funeral approached, slowly progressing down a street, I would stand still, doff my cap and drop my head.

But the past was slipping away. The hurdy-gurdy and the barrel organ were becoming rare and the muffin man had all but vanished from the streets. Only once did I hear the magic of the muffin bell. I did not understand what the ring meant until my mother pointed out the muffin man to me. He was then a curiosity. My mother told me that when she was young there were many of them. I fancy that at some time or another the bureaucrats banned the muffin bell – typical – but the bell of the Toni ice-

A brewery dray outside a public house. *(LMA)*

cream van was allowed. There were no Toni vans in those days but much in evidence were the Stop-Me-And-Buy-One Wall's ice-cream men. They were sited at strategic positions in the streets where they sat on their blue-and-white three-wheeled box cycles – now venerable antiques – to tempt us children as we passed by. Their rivals and predecessors, the Italian ice-cream men, were still on the streets with their timeless ice-cream barrows painted with swirling floral designs and covered by red-and-white-striped awnings supported by twisted brass columns. These were the picturesque hokey-pokey vendors, but my mother did not favour them, casting doubt on their cleanliness; their barrows did look old and battered, often needing paint. They were losing out and I bought my ice cream from the Wall's tricycle men.

Common still at that time were the rag-and-bone men. They alone still had a street cry, a cry of some poignant beauty. Recycling was a reality in those far-off days and they seemed to accept any rubbish. Sometimes they paid us boys in pennies, sometimes with sweets and sometimes with goldfish in a bowl.

Alas, today our city streets are bereft of this light humour of life. No longer do sheep wander the streets and bookies play hide-and-seek with policemen. Now even the trees have diminished. When I was a child Hackney boasted many trees but they seemed to give some offence to the local authority who, over the years, under one pretext or another, have chopped them down so that Hackney is no longer leafy.

The parish church of Hackney is St John's; its white baroque steeple sits incongruously on a plain classical body of grey brick. In the thirties the churchyard was peppered with decaying monuments and overhung by heavy trees, making it dark and gloomy. My father disliked it intensely – he felt death there. Today the trees have been felled and the tombstones moved to the edge of the churchyard. There is now a small pleasant green, a popular walkway for the people of Hackney.

My mother had no such inhibitions about the churchyard and walked me through it often to read the tombstones and see Blind Fred. I remember Blind Fred who, even while he lived, was a legend. Mother told me that he had been blind since birth. He was shabbily but neatly dressed in an overcoat and bowler hat, and sat all day long, in all weathers, in the depths of that gloomy churchyard, reading a Braille bible and selling matches and bootlaces. This he had done since his youth. 'He has to sell things,' said my mother, 'otherwise they would arrest him for begging.' But Blind Fred was never seen as a beggar. All treated him with respect, for he had become an institution, as much a part of Hackney as St John's church and the Hackney Empire. He was always cheerful. When we visited him my mother would say 'Put a penny in his box,' and this I always did. However, the day was to come when Blind Fred sat no longer in his place under the trees. He died when I was five in 1933. But he was not forgotten. A brass plaque was put up on the railings above where he had sat. One day my mother took me along to show me. On the plaque was inscribed: 'Hereby was seen for many years Blind Fred, a sunny soul.' Below was a biblical text in Braille: 'One thing I know, that whereas I was blind now I see.'

Another well-known character of Hackney was Dr Jelley, a mysterious man. I remember his strange surgery in Lower Clapton Road, which had a plate-glass window like a shop. In the window, on a red cloth, stood two brass candlesticks with a brass casket between them. Mauve velvet curtains concealed the surgery behind, or almost, for through a small gap I could just discern a gloomy interior that was too dark to reveal its secrets. The effect was weird and disturbing. It was more like a funeral parlour or a place for seances, than a surgery. My mother told me stories of this strange man.

Many years before, in the early years of the century when she was a child, he had been her doctor. He had a surgery just off the Roman Road, not far from Beale Place. My mother remembered him visiting his patients on horseback. 'He was the only doctor Nan could afford,' she told me.

'He didn't make much. He only charged sixpence a visit and gave a boy threepence to hold his horse.' She smiled. 'He was quite a sight, dressed like a huntsman in a top hat and a long black frock coat. He had riding boots, too, and wore one of those funny winged collars. He looked like Neville Chamberlain.' My mother paused and searched her memory. 'I remember he didn't have a doctor's bag. He just stuffed his instruments in his pockets. You could see them hanging down.' My mother shook her head. 'He was a rude man and told the truth straight out. He told Nan that her children should eat more meat and vegetables. No doubt he was right but she could not afford it. But he was a good doctor and kind to the poor. Sometimes he didn't charge them at all.' Then my mother adopted a mysterious tone. 'Mind you, some said he wasn't a proper doctor at all. And he got into trouble for carrying out an operation he shouldn't have and I think a woman died. They sent him to prison for that.' My mother did not expand on the nature of the operation, nor would I have understood if she had, for I guess now that it was an abortion. Despite this my mother told me that everyone thought highly of Dr Jelley as a people's doctor and remembered him with affection. Dr Jelley's past was indeed obscure. He had

been a medical student, but his qualifications were the subject of dark rumours. Mother doubted whether he was ever a doctor. He disappeared during the war without leaving a trace.

Hackney Empire is still with us. In those days before the war it flourished. Each Saturday the crowds would flock in. Being poor, our family could only afford 'the gods', so we would labour up a dark and seemingly endless spiral staircase, exhausted before we reached our destination. On entering 'the gods' we were greeted with the odours of peeled oranges and monkey nuts that provided sustenance and amusement for the under-privileged. Sometimes Max Miller or Arthur Askey would

The Hackney Empire, a fantasy of Edwardian baroque. *(LMA)*

appear at the Empire. I remember Arthur Askey well. I had heard him on the radio show *Band Waggon* as 'big-hearted Arthur' and supposed, as many others did, that he was a big man. It was a shock and a disappointment to see how small he was in reality. But Arthur Askey was only too aware of the situation, and as he pranced on stage he opened his jacket, threw out his chest and exclaimed, 'That's all there is of me folks.' And we all laughed. Then he did his famous bird song and we laughed some more.

But Max Miller and Arthur Askey apart, the turns were run-of-the-mill affairs. I found many of the acts tedious and longed for the end of the performance. When my parents were not looking, I relieved my boredom by surreptitiously dropping orange peel and peanut shells on the affluent seated in the expensive stalls below. I was not alone in this pastime, for the management had put up a notice forbidding it. Alas, eventually they killed off this simple fun by placing a long and narrow net under the gallery.

After the war the audiences dropped as the cinema became more popular. Sad days came when the Empire became a bingo palace and lost those unlikely towers. But now fortune smiles again and it has all been restored, the towers are back and so is the music hall.

There were fairs in Hackney in the thirties for there were still places to hold them. One was held on the site of the present town hall. Another was held on the Hackney Marshes, by the River Lea, just opposite the Robin Hood pub. These were real steam fairs, dirty and dusty, full of bustling crowds and rough entertainment: the boxing booths, the bearded lady and the dwarfs, the helter-skelter, the steam swings and the roundabouts. Some of these sights are still to be seen in the fairs of today. But the boxing booths, that test of male virility, and the exhibition of grotesque human forms have gone in these more refined days.

The interior of the Hackney Empire, showing the auditorium, the side of the stage, and the boxes. *(LMA)*

The cinemas were booming in the thirties and were scattered along the length of Mare Street. Some were old theatres like the Pavilion and Empress. Others like the Regal were new, built in that unique, once forgotten and despised style of art deco – the style of the twenties and thirties – the true style, I like to think, of the twentieth century. The glossy art deco seemed to be the way the world was going then, but the war changed the direction of development. We queued outside these cinemas of a Saturday night for the latest films. Posters outside advertised the programme. The one I remember was outside the Pavilion and was of the sinuous Jessie Matthews, apparently poured into a sleek long evening dress, tossing something over her shoulder.

I remember but few of the shops on Mare Street. There was certainly the Woolworths where everything was sold for threepence or sixpence. The time came when, as they grew more ambitious with their stock, problems arose with the more expensive items. Woolworths solved this problem ingeniously. So it was that, when I bought my first camera from them, I paid 6*d* for the front, 6*d* for the back and 6*d* for the film: 1*s* 6*d* altogether.

Hackney Pavilion. It was here that I saw Jessie Matthews in the film *Evergreen*. *(Hackney Archives)*

War and inflation swept this residue of the penny bazaar away. Hackney's department store was the long-established Matthew Rose, for me the most boring shop in Hackney, piled high with dreary clothes. It was replaced by Marks & Spencer's, only a marginal improvement in those days.

The shop I remember most vividly was Spokes the draper and haberdasher, a Hackney institution. I visited it frequently. Not that I was hung on haberdashery – far from it. No, my interest was in the curious arrangements made for payment. An assistant would put the money and bill into a little wooden bomb and hook it on to an overhead wire. A spring-loaded lever was pulled and the wooden bomb was sent whizzing along over the heads of the customers. On a good day the air hummed with these tethered overhead projectiles, which would meet in a kind of Clapham Junction at the cash desk. It was more exciting than a model railway. I was fascinated and made special visits to Spokes merely to watch this spectacle. Alas, this system, surely Victorian, has passed away with the coming of the colourless computer. Come to think of it, Spokes has passed away too, which is a shame.

These were the days when the Hackney version of art deco appeared in the furniture shops. The local cabinet-makers – there were many in Hackney –

Henry Spokes, draper's shop, Lower Clapton Road, 1939. It was a much loved institution that seemed to have been there forever, but it is now alas closed. (*Hackney Archives*)

went to town and produced strange inharmonious concoctions of wood, chrome plate and glass. Peering through the plate glass windows of Drage's, I saw dining-room tables that rested on two wooden walls rather than on four legs; sideboards made of white wood with shining chrome handles; coffee tables that balanced on a single pillar; and chrome tubular chairs. It all glittered and shone. Light winked from fan-like mirrors and danced on chrome and bleached oak. My father was impelled to imitate the style and I still have a sideboard, a coffee table and a lamp standard that he made.

Near home was a small group of neighbourhood shops in that short section of Frampton Park Road that lies between Darnley Road and Paragon Road. It was handy for shopping and these shops gave the area a village-like character. On the corner with Darnley Road was a cook shop, a utilitarian dining-room. Rough men, the lower class of worker and the unemployed, frequented it. Once, when I summoned up enough courage to look inside, I saw them seated, shabbily dressed, at light-brown pews eating simple meals: pre-cooked meat pies, jellied eels and the like.

Next door was a Jewish baker who sold delicious bread, at least if bought new. But when mother sent me there I was given instructions to buy a yesterday's loaf, which was a farthing cheaper. 'Anyway,' she said, 'new bread is indigestible.'

A Hackney shop in the 1930s. (LMA)

My special interest was in the sweet shop, where I bought large bottles of Tizer, my favourite drink, and old-fashioned sweets: sherbets, liquorice, candy sticks and, my favourites, humbugs and gobstoppers. Next door was a cycle shop that also recharged accumulators. The shopkeeper was black, a rarity in Hackney in those days, and he was married to a white woman. It was the topic of some gossip, but not much; some averred that it wasn't right. On the Paragon Road corner was a public house, noted for its large and fat publican. My father, who picked up bits of him after an air-raid, remarked that he was surprised at finding so very little left of such a large man.

On the other side of the road, at a corner opposite the pub, was an oil shop, so-called, I suppose, from the days of the oil lamp when paraffin oil would have been its main commodity. It was my least favourite shop for, among other things, it sold canes and one of my mother's punishments was to send me to the oil shop to buy one. Then it would be hung up in the kitchen as a threat. I can never remember the cane being used. Indeed, the time came when the mere threat of sending me out to buy a cane sufficed to bring me to order; I could not face that humiliation and the shopkeeper saying, 'Been a naughty boy again?' Whatever happened to those oil shops? Perhaps they metamorphosed into hardware emporia.

Adjacent was a dairy run by a Welsh couple, Mr and Mrs Jones. She had a short Welsh temper. Butter was piled into butter mountains and patted into shape, a charming operation to watch and one of the simple pleasures of those days. My mother bought Gouda cheese there and I have never lost the taste for this cheese, which must be eaten fresh to be at its best. Mrs Jones was always pressing us to buy milk from her, for there were milk wars in those days and she faced competition from the Express Dairy and United Dairies. I remember that their roundsmen plied us with inducements such as occasional free eggs and butter.

By the dairy was the obligatory fish and chip shop, notable for a pet 'talking' parrot. Or rather, it was said to talk – mainly it sat in its corner in sulky silence. On Fridays long queues stretched outside the shop. People came from all around, for the fish and chips were far superior to those of others in the trade. The proprietor attributed his success to cooking in oil – a rarity in those days – rather than dripping.

In the row of shops was a general grocer. His was an old-fashioned shop where most of the goods were sold loose and contained in brightly enamelled tin boxes that lined the shelves. Biscuits were weighed out from these boxes; broken biscuits were common and I bought these cheaply by the pennyworth as a treat. I would gaze at the grocer with fascination as he deftly weighed sugar into blue bags and tea into white ones. This simple shop had an atmosphere that exuded the mystery of those far-off places that yield such exotic goods as tea and coffee.

There were tensions between tradesmen at times. Once the Jewish baker, an irascible man, refused to serve me bread because I had bought a wrapped Hovis from the general grocers. 'You can get your white loaf from there, too!' He pointed across the road and I stole out, crestfallen, from his shop. I like to believe that he was not motivated by crass commercial jealousy, but objected to wrapped bread on aesthetic grounds. For the repair of shoes we went further afield, to Mr Southworth in Morning Lane, an old-fashioned cobbler with repaired shoes piled high in his window.

This shopping centre in Frampton Park Road has gone, destroyed by the same land mine that demolished 12 Darnley Road. Today children at the nearby school may wonder why there is a playground on both sides of Frampton Park Road. The truth is that it marks the 1940 blast area.

In the days just before the war change was in the air. With civic pride at its height the old Victorian Town Hall was demolished and the site changed into an ornamental garden. Behind it the new Town Hall rose from the waste ground where the old fair had been held. The old picturesque street lights of Hackney were torn down. They were lovely, tall lamps reaching to the sky, ending in a swirl of frilly cast-iron ornamentation with pendant globes of light beneath. They were replaced, alas, by ugly, concrete, tall, ill-balanced crookbacks, sinister cantilevered gallows that gave out a monochromatic yellow glare from sodium lighting. Traffic lights came to

Rising behind the remains of the old Victorian Town Hall, an imposing replacement is being constructed. Such was civic power in the 1930s. *(Hackney Archives)*

Hackney – strange that we could ever manage without them – and the Belisha beacons, those orange globes carried aloft on metal posts for all the world like giant toffee-apples. They aroused the curiosity and admiration of us boys; models of Belisha beacons appeared in the shops and I was given one for Christmas. Now they have passed away into history, giving way in Darwinian succession to zebra and pelican crossings.

Old Hackney was doomed. Just after the war the vicar, who looked like George Sanders (the actor), told us that he had seen the plans for Hackney. 'Hackney is going to be completely changed. You will never recognise the place.' Many who saw the plans came away with heavy hearts. The familiar was to go. What would the new be like?

The cosy slums in their friendly side streets have gone, either bombed by Hitler or rubbled during development. The horses have vanished from the streets and the trams no longer clank down Mare Street. But much still survives: St Luke's, St John's, the library and the old railway bridge that has spanned Mare Street since the railway age began. Best of all, Hackney Empire is once more a theatre and is flourishing.

Now Hackney is both familiar and foreign to me. When in Darnley Road there I stand, bemused, neither belonging nor not belonging, neither native nor stranger, partly lost and partly at home.

The grand new Hackney Town Hall. The old Town Hall has been completely demolished. (*Hackney Archives*)

4   *Victoria Park*

Victoria Park was a green oasis set in a desert of grey streets. To me it was a place of magic – the Kensington Gardens of the East End. I was taken to the park on Saturdays and Sundays. Saturday was the day of pilgrimage to my mother's parents in Bow. After a walk through drab streets, we crossed Hackney Common and entered Victoria Park by the Queen's Hotel. Tramlines ran by and there was a water trough nearby for the horses that once, but no longer, pulled the trams. The Queen's Hotel boasted an old-fashioned beer garden with green seats and green tables set amid greenery where children could sit with their parents. I remember once being taken there on a hot summer's day and being given a lemonade. It was my idea of heaven. But generally I was satisfied by a brightly coloured prism of ice bought from a Wall's Stop-Me-and-Buy-One.

The park was speckled with ponds and lakes large and small and we made for my favourite – the wild lake overhung by shade-giving trees. It had a rural aspect with muddy paths and natural banks and provided a refuge for living creatures. Mother would take me there and we would sit on a grassy bank and gaze at the lake. Water lilies languished on its dark surface and insects skimmed low above the waters. Ducks fed on the waterweed.

Alas, a year or two before the war this rustic scene was destroyed by the LCC. The trees were dynamited and the muddy banks made firm with concrete. The lake became neat and sterilised. It was partly filled in and construction began on a sophisticated concert bandstand, the so-called Tea Pavilion. It was in the art deco style with a large semi-circular glazed projection that faced the lake and, backing on to the far end, a bandstand, facing outwards, open to the air. The bandstand, a plain proscenium-arch affair, stood on the edge of a circular open-air dance floor.

The Tea Pavilion, constructed at such a cost, never saw a thirties tea dance, for war broke out just as it was completed. It was eventually opened on 7 May 1940, of all dates, as part of the LCC's 'Holidays at Home' campaign – an unnecessary incentive, to say the least, as a few days later the Germans invaded the Low Countries and northern France, making holidays abroad strictly for the intrepid only. The fashion for decorous tea dancing went out with the 1950s and in its turn the Tea Pavilion was rubbled and grassed over. The final result is that the old lake is now a little smaller than it was in Queen Victoria's reign.

Leaving the lake, we made for the splendid Victoria Fountain. No ordinary fountain, this, but a magnificent, if preposterous, monument to the goddess of water. The drinking fountain itself lay under an elaborate canopy soaring some 60 feet into the air; a capped octagonal structure of marked ecclesiastical appearance, not unlike a lady chapel. An array of marble-pointed arches rested on a circle of eight pink granite piers and carried a pointed cupola of Moorish fantasy. I looked at it in wonder. Under its groined vault, cherubs mounted sculptured dolphins: some were stationary white stone but others were a motley of lively street urchins. They clambered noisily over the edifice, clinging to the cherubs and dolphins. No wonder the fountain was battered by some sixty years of this rough affection. Nor, judging by their appearance, did these lively worshippers appreciate that the fountain was dedicated to the worship of water.

Water came from many artfully placed orifices: from urns held by four fat cherubs and from four taps sited between them. Four bronze cups were chained to the fountain. My mother pointed to inscriptions which affirmed the purity of water against more bacchanalian drinks. One read: 'Temperance is a bridle of gold.' It meant nothing to me. I often attempted to fill a cup for a drink, but my mother always stopped me. 'You don't know who's been using them,' she would say, looking around at the dirty tramps and the filthy ragamuffins. Then, as if to confirm her suspicions,

The new Tea Pavilion, the building of which involved the felling of many trees. This art deco structure was symbolic of the aspirations of the 1930s. It has now been demolished. (LMA)

The Victoria (Burdett-Coutts) Fountain in Victoria Park, in the 1930s. Mother and I visited it every Saturday afternoon when we went to see her parents in Bow. *(LMA)*

an unsteady tramp would sidle up and sip the waters of temperance, and I'd run down the broad steps of the fountain on to the grass, glad to be away from its oppressive presence. Today the park's fountains have gone and it is as dry as the desert.

Finally our Saturday walk would take us to the canal, and sometimes we would watch great shire horses pulling barges. Then we crossed at Gunmakers Lane – where bronze cannon were once made – into Bow to visit my grandmother.

The Lido, like the Tea Pavilion, was another manifestation of the 1930s. It was built, open to the sky, in subdued streamlined forms, a paradise of sun and water with a sleek new architecture of gleaming tiles and shining chrome. Diving boards, tall curving scaffolds of chrome, dominated its blue clear waters: a world of leisure and not of work. The sun always seemed to be shining in those days, or perhaps we only went along on fine days when I swam with my father. I enjoyed it so much better than the claustrophobic Hackney baths.

The Lido reflected social change: men were allowed to swim topless and mixed bathing was allowed two days a week and at the weekends! But at a price. There was a charge of sixpence for such exciting prospects, whereas single-sex swimming was free. In those days the Lido shone brightly as a watery dreamland, but the future belied the promise for the Lido was to lose its magic. The war came and it became a dismal static water tank to serve the firefighters. It revived after the war but in the jet age, where we glory in the sun of foreign parts, it declined into oblivion. Now it has been filled in for use as a car park.

On Sunday mornings my father would take me to see the model boats. Even now the smell of meths brings back memories of those far-distant days. The aroma was exuded from model steamboats that men played with on the ponds. Watching these activities became a frustrating experience, for the boats were rarely to be seen steaming across the surface. Mostly, they were to be found high and dry, half hidden in the bordering trees, upended where their enthusiastic owners pored over them, examined them minutely, tinkered with them and readjusted their innards. Even when these steamboats were actually on the water they rarely sailed but remained immobile by the water's edge, where their besotted owners vainly endeavoured to raise steam and get the engines turning over. When in luck, there would be an all-too-brief voyage, then it was back to dry dock. Sometimes there were races, not with the model steamboats but with noisy petrol engine jobs tethered to a central stake. One followed the other in endless circular journeys, to my intense boredom.

Before long I would turn my attention to the model yachts. These were an elegant species and I watched their soothing voyages for some time. They sailed gracefully across the pond, heeling with style as the wind

caught them. They were beautiful; true models scaled down from the real thing, resplendent with detail as behoves true thoroughbreds. There were miniature cabins, lockers and life belts. They sported graceful sails. I saw a plethora of fine cords for the control of rudders and sails. I yearned to possess one. My father bought me a cheap substitute that wallowed helplessly on the lake. He lightened it by scooping out its solid hull. So modified, it sailed out swiftly to the middle of the pond and there sank – the hull was leaky.

After leaving the model-boat pond we would go to watch the kite-flyers: men and boys of all ages and their kites of all shapes and sizes – box kites,

The Lido, Victoria Park, a scene from the pre-jet age. My father often took me there for a swim in the summer. It has since been filled in and the site is used as a car park. *(LMA)*

The boating lake, Victoria Park. The pagoda, damaged in the war, was subsequently demolished. *(LMA)*

trapezoid kites and simple makeshift kites. Some were so large that they required sophisticated winches to tether them to the ground; alas, when men get involved in anything simplicity seems to go out of the window. Hour after hour the kite-flyers would play with their kites, making them go higher and higher and sending paper messages up the tethering string. Once I decided to enter the fray with a small paper kite, but I was soon dissatisfied with it against the sophistication of the silk giants. My father thought that he could do better. He designed a large kite – a good solid job – constructed with a heavy wooden frame and aerofoil surfaces of a tough oilskin fabric. It looked impressive, but it was too heavy to fly. Today in my mind's eye I can still picture the scene with the kites fluttering against a sky dominated by St Augustine's – a church that is no longer there. This was the end of our Sunday morning in Victoria Park. We would leave, as always, for my grandmother's and the lunch we called Sunday Dinner.

5 Saturday & Sunday

Weekends were all the same: family affairs, given over to such rites as visiting grandparents and taking walks in the parks. On sunny days we did not jump into cars and drive to the coast like motorised lemmings, for no one in our class could afford such luxuries, nor did we desire them.

In those days society was compact. The humble ambitions of the poor made it unnecessary for them to seek esoteric occupations miles from their homes. Any job nearby would do. The absence of motor cars limited the physical bounds of their social life and they married boys or girls of the neighbourhood. Sons and daughters, grandsons and granddaughters, nieces and nephews all lived close to each other.

We were no exception and my grandparents lived no great distance away. Visiting them was part of the clockwork routine of our weekly life.

Grandfather Wilson in his prime and Grandmother Wilson, Granny, in her prime. (*Author's collection*)

My father's parents were but a few streets away. As my mother's lived in Bow the journey there was more adventurous, as we had to cross Victoria Park, that island of green in the grey ocean of the vast city. There was a regular time for visits to these relatives: in addition to visiting my mother's parents on Saturday afternoon, we went to my father's on Sunday morning. This order of things remained as unchanging as that of the moon's orbit about the earth. No departure from it was permitted.

But I had Saturday mornings to myself. Saturday mornings! A time of freedom! Free of parents, free of relatives and free of schoolmasters! The tyranny of the school was over and that of the relations had yet to begin. The sense, the happy sense, of freedom was very great and that emotion, born then, is still carried within me. It often returns.

So on Saturday morning off I would go to the tuppenny rush. What memories that brings. I joined the unruly mob gathering at the side entrance of the Empress cinema in Mare Street. We were a joyful lot buoyed by the riches of carefree happiness. We had not a care in the world as we scuffled and pushed against the locked doors. Life was good, and yet . . . and yet an outside observer would have seen nothing more than a press of shoddily dressed children, poor, not very clean and no doubt smelly, shouting and pushing each other. But I suppose we had more happiness with our tuppences than the richer children of today with their television sets and computer games.

As the opening time drew near excitement grew to fever pitch and the scuffling and pushing intensified. We could hardly bear the tension and demanded entry with good-humoured shouts. When the bolts were drawn and the doors flung open, we entered with the abandon of a desperate storming party; disorganised, yelling and fighting, shoving our way to our seats armed with pop and bags of sweets. Looking back over the years I wonder how the management survived it, and even more why they ever staged an event so trying to their nerves and damaging to the fabric of the cinema, for the tuppenny rush was not a passive affair where children, all neat and trim, merely went along to the cinema to watch films. There was positive spectator participation and the film show was but a part of the general entertainment. Included in the rich pageant of the tuppenny rush was meeting other children, talking to them, shouting at them, pushing them, eating and drinking, roaring encouragement to the unresponsive heroes of the films and booing the equally unresponsive villains. The soundtrack of a film was supplemented by the noise of cracking nuts, the popping of fizz bottles and active vocal participation in the action.

The films, apart from the cartoons, were serials. In all of them the American Dream emerged victorious against its enemies: Red Indians, bad men and shyster lawyers. Its knights errant were Rin-Tin-Tin, the wonder dog, and various cowboys. Oddly, I only remember one of those films in any detail, the first I saw, which was an odd mixture of cowboy and science fiction; the cowboy hero was none other than the great Tom Mix. Some advanced, but malign, civilisation has buried itself deep in a vast underground city below some western American desert. Why it should have done this escapes me. It is surprising that this advanced civilisation is so interested in the arid desert above. Nor can I recollect the cause of conflict with Tom Mix. I suppose that they must be up to no good, otherwise Tom Mix would not have to deal with them. I remember underground lifts, marvels rather like those in today's Hilton and Hyatt hotels. At the end of the serial a death ray, a pulsed laser we would call it now, gets out of hand and destroys the underground city of this civilisation. I watched with horror as the marvellous underground city melted. Tom Mix and the heroine get away just in the nick of time. Once again the American Dream triumphs.

My maternal grandparents, with Mother in between. (*Author's collection*)

I suppose we children were pleased with the result, although looking back I think it was a pity that Tom Mix was not melted down rather than the interesting civilisation. Apart from that film I can only remember Rin-Tin-Tin and Gene Autry with his guitar. Gene Autry with his smooth features and Brylcreemed hair was no favourite of mine; I preferred more rugged heroes. He bored my mates and me with his singing and strumming through numerous serials. But, perhaps, it was better than nothing.

Too soon the tuppenny rush was all over and we children dispersed rather quietly to our homes for dinner. The rest of my weekend was spoken for.

Aunt Nell. She read to me a mixture of Dr Johnson, Fanny Burney and *Just William. (Author's collection)*

Saturday afternoon, the time of the pilgrimage to my mother's parents, the Prudens, was to 13 Beale Place in Bow where I was born. We called it Nan's, not Granddad's for, as far as my grandparents were concerned, ours was a matriarchal society. There we would drink strong tea with sterilised milk, which kept for days in those times when refrigerators were a luxury.

On Sunday I would go to Gran's in 17 Stevens Avenue a few roads away for Sunday lunch, always a fine beef roast. It was a small flat and the family lived for the most part in the kitchen. There were five of us, Dad, Granny, Aunt Nell, Grandpa and me crammed into that tiniest of kitchens; a kitchen that served as a dining-room and general living-room.

I would look around. The centre-piece was a shining black Kitchener, where stacked coals glowed from their tiny prison, heating hob, oven and kitchen. On the hob was a collection of bright black iron pots. A gleaming brass kettle stood on the hearth. Above, there was a mantelpiece clut-tered with ornaments Victorian-style, and draped with a green beaded mantel cloth. On both sides of the mantelpiece were bracket gas lamps no longer used but a reminder of the gas age. On one side of the fireplace was a dresser displaying a dinner and tea service of crinkled pink and red china, some antique kitchen scales and a silver-plated teapot that Uncle Wilby gave my grandparents as a wedding present long, long ago. It was never used. There was a rocking chair, an object of curiosity. I wanted to use it but was forbidden because it was Grandpa's and Grandpa was in it. I glowered.

One day I found under the dresser, behind concealing curtains, a curious green ceramic object, shaped like a bowl but with sides that sloped over to form a cover with a hole in the centre. It was a spittoon. 'Horrible thing,' said my aunt in reply to my enquiry. 'Granny won't have it. She says the place is not a pub.' I remembered the notice in the trams. 'Spitting prohibited. Penalty £5.'

'Can I go into the front room and sit on the furniture, Gran?' The front room was a holy of holies only used on Sundays and at Christmas, and even I was not brash enough to crash into that room uninvited. On hearing a 'yes and be careful' I dashed along the landing. I heard Aunt Nell cry out 'Do watch the lino!' as she pursued me. A heavy aroma of church polish greeted me as I pushed open the door. The room smelt of Sunday and sanctity. The floor was covered by linoleum that Gran had polished to a glassy finish and I could see myself quite clearly in it when I peered down.

There was a scattering of rugs, and landing on one I tobogganed along waving my arms in a vain attempt to keep my balance. I somersaulted on to the floor. I laughed but it hurt. It was not the first time and would not be the last. Aunt Nell was full of concern as she pulled me up. 'I did tell you to be careful. I'm always telling Mum not to polish it so.'

The front room was spotless; a cold room that had the air of not being lived in. In one corner was an aspidistra, its leaves dark and brightly polished. In the centre was a mahogany dining-room table polished to a mirror finish. It was only used for special occasions, Sunday tea and Boxing Day dinner. The other furniture was quiescently High Victorian. There was a black elaborate china cabinet full of ornaments and a tiered mantelpiece covered with porcelain vases. Each Sunday I asked my aunt, 'Can I look at the ornaments?', which meant she had to take them down so that I could inspect them one by one. I was particularly taken by a red and white Bohemian scent bottle. 'Can I have it when you die, Gran?' Years later,

One of Great Uncle Albert's pubs, the Avenue. *(Author's collection)*

when Gran lay in her coffin by her window, Aunt Nell gave it to me. 'You always wanted it,' she said.

Gran would come in and sit down on an upright chair by the window. There she enjoyed her favourite occupation – watching the world go by. The streets were full of happenings in those days, so that Gran would spend most of her day seated openly in her front window watching the daily pageant. It was the 1930s equivalent of the modern TV soap opera. Often she commented on what she saw: 'There goes Mrs Walsh. I wonder what she's doing out this time of the day. . . . Those boys are kicking their ball against Mr Smith's wall again. He will be cross. . . . Oh. Mr Smith's coming out. He's chasing them away.' This was the Mr Smith who always kept a sharp lookout for the passing horses and what they might deposit. On those lucky occasions he would rush from his house with a shovel and collect this valuable manure. He acted as if he had commoners' rights. 'Here comes the milkman, he's late today.' The milkman came with his churn on a cart pulled by a donkey. Milk was ladled into jugs: unhygienic and soon to be banned.

Another long-running saga for her viewing was that of the street bookie – Bert. In the days before betting shops the street bookie fulfilled the need of the working man who liked a flutter. But unlike betting on the course or at the Tote, street betting was illegal and the street bookie lived a precarious life. Bert knew his business and would post two lookouts at each

Another of Great Uncle Albert's pubs, the Prince of Wales. Mann, Crossman and Paulin's are now a long-forgotten brewery. (*Author's collection*)

end of the avenue while he took bets. Thus, when the majesty of the law
made an entrance Bert made his exit. But once the law got cunning and a
pincer movement trapped Bert in Stevens Avenue with no exit. In his
desperation Bert knocked feverishly on a friendly door, which opened. He
dashed through the house into the back yard and over the fence. All this
added to the fun and the citizens of the street gossiped about this incident
for months after. These were the simple pleasures of the poor.

Gran had a brother Albert, who came from the same respectable mould
as her. Once I went to Walthamstow to visit him and his wife in their large
detached house. He had got on in the world and looked the part. I
remember him as a Galsworthian character, short and well-filled, dressed in
a brown suit with waistcoat. Across his
bulging middle was draped a gold watch and
chain, which is what I mainly remember of
him. He exuded the solid self-satisfaction of
one who has done well in life by his own
efforts. I felt he must be one of the immortals
– yet he was dead within a year. Great Uncle
Albert had made money. As a lad he had
perception. Every morning he would take
down the shutters of a small sweet shop for a
lonely old lady and each evening put them up
again. He did this for nothing. When she died
she left him the shop and everything else she
had. After a time he bought a small pub, the
Avenue Arms in Walthamstow, selling Taylor
Walker's beers and Barley Mow ales. He
prospered, and bought another pub, the
Prince of Wales, of that long-lost brewery
Mann, Crossman and Paulin's. He invested
wisely and was accounted wealthy in our
circle.

He tried to help his brother and sister, but
without much success. Brother Bill, Great
Uncle Bill, was a character of a type that does
not exist today. Whereas his brother was the
symbol of solid Victorian lower middle-class
respectability, Uncle Bill was the reverse. He
was a Victorian card. His exuberance shone
from a piratical face full of humorous malice.
He was a joker, sometimes a malevolent joker.
Once after a row with his wife he gave her his
weekly pay packet in farthings. She burst into

Great Uncle Bill, the generous wastrel.
(*Author's collection*)

tears. But mostly he was a ragged-trousered philanthropist using Uncle Albert's money. First Uncle Albert financed him in a fish and chip shop but Bill gave away his fish and chips to the poor children. Next Uncle Albert set him up in a sweet shop – but Bill gave away sweets and ice-cream to the needy children of east London. At this point Albert washed his hands of him. After all this Uncle Albert tried to help set Granny up in a pub, for she was an experienced Victorian barmaid and had helped him in his ventures. But Grandpa would have none of it. Both Granny and Aunt Nell were bitter about this and attributed Grandpa's decision to his excessive caution. Maybe they were right, but I often think that it was his silent stubborn pride.

Before Sunday dinner I read my comics. They were old-fashioned comics that Aunt Nell had bought me: *Tiger Tim*, *Chips* and *Film Fun*. They were not easy to read for, as well as the antics of the cartoon characters, there were balloons of speech and captions in small print underneath. I was caught on the horns of a dilemma: which do I read first – the story text or the balloons of speech above? As a matter of fact, you could get the story by reading one or the other; the text need not be read at all – but being conscientious I read it anyway.

'Tired Tim' and 'Weary Willie' featured in *Chips*, as they had been doing for half a century. The story line was always the same: how to get something for nothing. The comic effort of this pair of layabouts to avoid work always ended in disaster, so I suppose there was a moral there, but I derived chief pleasure not from the dismal endings but from the work-shy ingenuity of the pair. The cartoon had started in late Victorian times and the theme of avoiding work seemed to fly in the face of Victorian values. Or was it a lack of knowledge of the true cause of unemployment in those days: that men did not loaf about from choice but were the victims of Victorian market forces?

Film Fun, of course, featured film stars, an ingenious idea to have ready-made characters. All in all, these comics lacked the direct bouncy style of *Dandy* and *Beano* that appeared just before the war and became my preferred choice. They did away with the story text and so were much easier to read than *Tiger Tim* and *Comic Cuts*. And the characters were bold and appealed to boys, none more so than the backwoods Superman, Desperate Dan, perpetually half-shaved and invincibly tough. No steamroller ever flattened him and any motor car that crashed into him bounced off and was left a shattered wreck. There were other boldly drawn characters: the cheeky Corky the Cat, and Lord Snooty, who proved that the upper classes could be fun.

After dinner my aunt and I would settle down and she would read me passages from Richmal Crompton's *William* and tell me stories of family history. She was a superb raconteuse. But there were sometimes readings from more weighty works: Boswell's *Life of Johnson*, Fanny Burney's *Evelina*,

Pepys's *Diary* and *Gulliver's Travels*. My aunt was imbued with the history of those times. The past was her refuge from the present.

I accepted this mixed diet from my aunt with equanimity. Of the authors, I preferred Richmal Crompton. What boy would not? Of course, as a boy I identified with the intrepid William; a born leader, whose flair for ingenious mischief made my natural mischief appear quite tame. I admired his great talent for lateral thinking and plausible excuses for misbehaviour. Unconsciously my hairstyle, if you can call my confused jumble of hair a style, resembled that of William and so did the generally dishevelled state of my clothes. So much so that when I went to a bookshop to buy a *William* book the shopkeeper called out, 'William's come to collect his book!'

Only vaguely did I recognise that William inhabited a different world from mine. He lived in a detached house in a green village with its country parsonage and grand houses. His father was a wealthy businessman and the household boasted a cook and a maid. My circumstances were somewhat different. Grey streets were substitutes for green fields and our basement flat hardly compared with his detached house. And even the Hubbles lacked a maid. But somehow these distinctions meant little to me.

While Aunt Nell was reading me a *William* story a call would come: 'Nell, Reggie's ready.' It was Mrs Bart calling from downstairs. It was time for Sunday school. My heart would drop. I remember all the Sunday schools as merged into one long Sunday afternoon of boredom. The teaching was mainly of the 'gentle Jesus meek and mild' variety. Mr Boniface was the Sunday school superintendent and had a wife of delicate Pre-Raphaelite appearance. Mr Boniface had notions of democracy and formed a committee of the pupils to come up with suggestions. I was the favourite of a Miss Cooper, a sweet middle-aged spinster who was our teacher, so I went on the committee. We were asked to suggest a hymn. So each week, with a single-minded purpose, I advocated the hymn 'Holy, Holy, Holy'. It was turned down regularly. In the end, by my grinding persistence, I had my way and it was sung one evening. It was my one and only contribution. After that I was silent.

One Christmas Mr Boniface decided to mount a tableau of children to represent that ever-fresh story of the angel of the Lord surprising the three shepherds watching their flocks on Christmas night. This event was to be staged before a full audience in the new Institute. Half a dozen or so children were selected to make up the tableau. I was one of them; Mr Boniface, for the sake of keeping peace, deemed it better to have me within rather than vocally protesting without. Roles were assigned according to sex: the earthy shepherds were to be boys and the ethereal angels girls; this was by mutual consent, for none of the boys wanted to be angels.

The biblical text had to be modified in order to obtain a balance between the sexes, for although the Bible story has a number of shepherds there is but one angel of the Lord. So the angel was pluralised and three girls chosen. Doris Tucker, my childhood sweetheart, was among them. The girls were pinched little things with runny noses, so typical of East End girls of the day, and anything less cherubic would be difficult to imagine. If there was an abundance of angels of the Lord, then there was a shortage of sheep. The flock over which the shepherds watched was represented by just one stuffed sheep. Clearly, the audience was going to need some imagination.

Although it is not easy to imagine the girls as divine angels, at least they gave no trouble. The same could not be said of the three boys chosen as shepherds: Dicky Drage, Jimmy Thomas and me. We were all pushy and the central message of Christmas, peace on earth and goodwill to all men, was alien to our way of thinking. A power struggle was inevitable once it became apparent that some shepherds were going to be more equal than others.

The shepherds' perks consisted of the shepherd's crook and the single stuffed sheep. At first I gave them little thought but then at the first rehearsal quick-witted Dicky Drage snatched the shepherd's crook. I was losing out. I made a grab for the crook and grasped it at one end but I was unable to wrest it from him. The struggle ended when Mr Boniface unfairly – in my eyes anyway – awarded the crook to Dicky Drage. He admonished me, 'Will you never learn to behave yourself?', adding insult to injury. I was mortified and while in this state Jimmy Thomas seized the opportunity to grab the solitary sheep. Again too late, I contested its possession and once again Mr Boniface ruled against me. I was left with nothing but a sense of extreme deprivation. This arrangement persisted throughout rehearsals despite my frequent appeals of 'It's my turn.' But I considered rehearsals as one thing, the performance another. I was determined on a coup.

Come the night, and as the curtain went up and the tableau was revealed to the audience, I made my move and grabbed the sheep by its tail. I pulled hard at the tail as Jimmy Thomas held on to the body. We were oblivious of the audience as the tableau, supposedly stationary, swayed in the struggle. As the pulling and the twisting continued, the connection between tail and sheep weakened. Suddenly I became aware of the audience beginning to giggle. But I kept my hold on the tail. I was determined to keep my share of the action. I started to fiddle with the tail, rotating it clockwise and anti-clockwise. Then it parted company from the rest of the sheep. I was left holding a short woolly tail. But in the moment of my triumph I panicked. I realised I had damaged the sheep and tried desperately to repair it. I pushed the tail hard on to the main body of the sheep. It fell off. I tried to intertwine the parted strands of tail and sheep. It did not work. I persisted. I tried again and again but without success. So absorbed was I that I forgot there was an audience of some two hundred watching me and tittering. They were enjoying my performance. Then, suddenly overwhelmed by remorse, I let the tail drop to the floor.

After Sunday school came a brief spell of freedom. We boys – I recall no girls in the group – gathered together and then wandered down to a little sweet shop known as Curtis's, to spend our halfpennies. It was run by an old lady, Miss Curtis, whose 'sweet shop' was no more than a passageway in her house. I think that after the war it succumbed to officialdom and legislation, but a more sympathetic world allowed her a scant living and gave us boys much pleasure. We always preferred to buy sweets from Curtis's rather than shops, because she was sympathetic to boys, unlike the shopkeepers who regarded us as no more than a necessary nuisance. In the dark, cramped little passage we watched her dispense highly coloured 'suckers' and break up a tray of cream toffee into ha'p'orths using a little hammer.

After we left Curtis's we would gossip until the pangs of hunger assailed us. It was time for Sunday tea. Sometimes I took home uninvited guests for my mother to feed. Sometimes I descended on other boys' homes for tea. Then came the most depressing part of Sunday, getting ready for evening church. Attending Sunday church was the price we paid for joining in its social life.

The church in those days was not the church of today. Today our churches are lively places where we have our services by the light of the bright morning so that we may get away in our cars to the coast on a summer's day. The priests are dressed in colourful, some would say garish, robes. The air is suffused with lively renderings of the latest copyrighted hymns selected from, perhaps, too many hymn books. They are difficult to hold in just one hand. The twang of a guitar is heard in the air, not to mention the drum, trumpet and tambourine. The congregation sways and sings with charismatic abandon. It is a friendly place and near the end of the service we walk around clasping hands saying 'God be with you'. Once an old lady was heard to say that she did not go to church to be friendly but to worship her God. I know what she meant.

When I was a boy churches were most properly sombre. They were stuffy and there was little joy in them. St Luke's was no exception. It was a dark Victorian church of frozen Gothic. I remember only the winters when we went to church in the gloom of the evening and the most popular service of the day was held. Ours was a broad church and the clergyman, never called a priest, dressed in plain black with a white surplice. We too were dressed in our Sunday best in all the range of shades from dark grey to black. None would wear – or even contemplate wearing – jacket and flannels, let alone lumber jackets and jeans, with country shirts and no ties.

As I entered between my parents I was engulfed by the all-embracing gloom and drowned by the swelling dirge of the organ. There was a heavy oppressive smell, not of incense but of over-applied furniture polish. To me this smell became synonymous with holiness. Soon we were singing uncopyrighted hymns from the *Ancient and Modern*, with respect if not with joy. The sound from the mighty organ overwhelmed our feeble voices and submerged us like some tremendous tidal wave. More boring than the hymns were the chanted psalms. The grey gloom, the cloying organ sound, this holy smell and the indescribable boredom were oppressive to my spirit. I felt trapped in sound, darkness and odour. Even to this day I cannot but think of those evenings without sinking into an unpleasant depressive stupor.

My father always selected a pew in the darkness of the far end of the church. We huddled in the gloom of this obscure corner where we felt secure against the general happenings elsewhere. My father brought comics along for me to read to relieve the worst effects of ennui, and also something for me to suck to alleviate my ever-present pangs of hunger. Even these palliatives did not suffice. During the turgid and turbid sermon, which went on interminably, the boredom became painful. I tried to lift my spirits by switching the handbags of the ladies in front of our pew. When they left they evinced no surprise and automatically crossed over to take the right bags. They said nothing. They were used to me. At last the ritual of passing the plate came round and I heaved a sigh of relief; the end was near. I was always expected to put a penny in the plate and once caused a minor scandal when, down to my last penny, I took a ha'penny change to buy some suckers at Curtis's after the service. 'It makes sense to me,' I told my father. But he did not appreciate my logic.

With Sunday evening the unchanging cycle of the week was complete. Sunday was the epitome of the sameness that characterised my childhood life but, though bored by it, I did not rebel against it.

6   *Morning Lane School*

I was sent to school at the age of four and went eagerly, perhaps because as an only child I looked forward to the comradeship. On my first day I remember being walked by my mother along the Hackney streets. I was dressed in the style of a little boy in the thirties. I wore short trousers that ended just above the knee and long woollen socks that reached to just below the knee. Over a long-sleeved shirt I wore a sleeveless pullover. After a few minutes' walk we came to a gaunt building built in a formidable and intimidating style – Victorian Institutional. This was Morning Lane School. I gazed at it with growing dismay. I felt small and insignificant.

The school was a tall building of red brick with an array of sharply pointed stone gables, its manner stern and authoritarian. It stood in its own grounds, alas not the gracious grass sward of a public school, but the dark-grey asphalt of the London County Council. The exclusivity of the establishment was protected by encircling walls. Now walls can impart dignity to a building, but not these; their unaesthetic topping of broken glass embedded in stained concrete would have brought shame to a penal institution. This educational fortress was to be my alma mater for three years. Twenty years previously it had been my father's, and he had succeeded in winning a beautiful Art Nouveau certificate that testified to his scriptural knowledge.

Mother and I joined a queue of boys and girls waiting for entry into the school; for some reason we had to queue outside. After standing for some time I grew bored and pushed the boy in front of me to see what would happen. He fell forward on the boy in front who also fell and the crocodile of children collapsed like a line of dominoes. I had not made a good start.

As mother guided me through the entrance my spirits drooped; I beheld a grim interior, as unwelcoming as the exterior. 'Drab' is too cheerful a word to describe the place. I saw walls painted in an oily and sickly yellow and woodwork varnished dark brown. I trod on floors stained grey by grime and speckled black with blobs of cheap ink. The place was a nocturne where the whole gamut of colours from dirty yellow to dull brown was explored, a scene that had not changed since the days of Queen Victoria. We children of the grey streets had also to endure the drabness of these dingy classrooms. Bright colours were unknown in our young lives.

I found myself sitting at a battered cast-iron and wooden bench, my mother gone. 'I'll fetch you for dinner, dear.' I was alone with forty other

The Art Nouveau certificate awarded to my father (Arthur Wilson) by the London County Council. *(Author's collection)*

children arranged in ordered rows of desks in a large, dimly lit room facing the teacher and her blackboard. It was all very strange. At the end of the morning my mother came and took me home for midday dinner. Then I was returned for afternoon school. There we were told to sleep. I rested my head on the hard wood of the desk but I could not sleep; my mind was too full of thoughts. At the end of school my mother was waiting by the gates to take me home. That was the end of the first day at school. I had mixed feelings.

I was to spend the next three years of my life in this institution. Of these years I retain for the most part only general impressions and recollections of repetitive events. Of specific happenings I remember but little. In my memory all lessons are blurred into one. The blackboard and easel dominated lessons and I copied down the teacher's dusty chalkings on a squeaky grey slate, which I found unpleasant both to the touch and to the ear. I much preferred pencil and paper. Of my scholastic achievements I remember nothing, except once when I was chided for forming the letter S the wrong way round. 'You're getting as bad as Jack. You can do better than that.' Jack, a rough, unkempt boy, was the acknowledged dim wit of the class who always wrote his 'S's back to front. I hung my head in shame at being graded with him. Apart from this, my only other educational memory was a poster in the entrance hall illustrating the four seasons. Spring was an umbrella, summer a bright, ray-emitting sun, autumn falling leaves and winter a snowman.

Once a week we children were gathered in the main hall and seated in a ring. This was to encourage conversation. But while other children prattled on, I sat dumb, listening in silence to all the small talk that went on around me. Perhaps it was because I was an only child, perhaps it was innate. (I have improved but little over the years.) The teachers grew worried at my silence. I was practically ordered to speak. 'Say something, Alan.' So prodded along one day, I turned to my neighbour and opened my first conversation: 'I have got a red motor car, have you?' After that I became too talkative.

The red motor car was a toy that had been made by my father. It worked quite well, but I was dissatisfied with the colour. I wanted blue. After all, the famous car of those days was Malcolm Campbell's record-breaking *Bluebird* and its fame had reached down even to young children. I asked my father to change the colour. Not wanting the bother, he countered this by telling me that before *Bluebird* there was another famous racing car, *The Scarlet Runner*. With this mythical car I was satisfied, and even boasted of it to my friends. Only many years later did I discover that it was a variety of runner bean.

Many of my childhood friends attended both Morning Lane School and St Luke's Church – it was a close society. Among them were Jimmy Thomas, Dickie Drage, Norman Norris, Lennie Fuller and, last but not least, Doris Tucker. The latter friendship, once close, did not last, for in those days little boys gravitated towards other little boys and little girls to other little girls.

My early school years were disturbed by a serious illness. I had been taken to see the circus for a treat before Christmas. It was the first time I had been to a circus but I did not enjoy it. I became tired during the performance and watched listlessly. I asked to go home.

At home I lay on a sofa and, feeling strangely exhausted, fell into an uneasy and fitful doze. The memory of that awful sick feeling remained with me for decades. Illogically I associated it with the circus, as if the circus was the cause of the malady. I refused to go to the circus again for several decades but I am now quite cured of that phobia. I saw the concern of my mother in her face for she never concealed her feelings. 'There's something wrong with the boy,' she told my father. 'Oh, it's nothing. The boy's tired.' But my mother's instinct was, as ever, right and my father's logic flawed. I had diphtheria, or 'dip' as it was commonly called.

After days of fever and fearful dreams I returned to the land of the living. I had escaped death again, just. I found myself in an alien place where strangers in blue and white garb attended me impersonally. No mother. No father. No one I knew. I felt abandoned. A day or two later in the evening the vicar came and I felt reassured. But why did my parents not come? In my longings I had visions of my mother, her head alone appearing and floating about the hospital ward.

Afterwards I found out that the authorities had told my parents that it would be unkind to visit me, as I would be upset after they left. In those days we were still in the aftermath of that unnatural Victorian age where natural reactions were regarded with abhorrence and when there was no shortage of people who were ready to give advice provided that it was hard and not too pleasant.

When I had recovered I left for a convalescent home. At first I did not like the home. I felt hemmed in by a crowd of other children, I wanted space and, although not alone, I felt lonely. But then a little girl befriended and comforted me. It is surprising how early the mothering instinct develops in girls. I began to enjoy living with other children and even being regimented.

We ate around a large scrubbed deal table and the other children made fun of the food and the lack of it. Food was sparse. We went hungry and I lost weight from my frail frame. I remember mainly potatoes-and-gravy for the midday meal. 'The nurses eat the meat,' I was told by other little boys. This dish was followed by milk puddings: tapioca, semolina and the like. At tea there were paste sandwiches: these were very neatly finished with the filling exactly in line with the edge of the bread. 'How do they do that?' I enquired. 'The nurses lick them,' I was told by more than one small voice.

In the depth of the winter we were thrust outdoors every day to play, even when sleet fell. It was alleged that this was good for us; perhaps it was. But my memory is that my nose was always running. Sometimes I would go to the locked iron gates and look out at the countryside that was spread below. They were the fields of freedom.

I was excited when a big box of toys came. 'They are for you,' the little girl said. I was surprised and pleased. The other children gathered round as I unpacked them. The little girl told me to share the toys, which I did reluctantly. Sharing was a new experience for me. But a strange happiness came to me as I did.

Although I was only at the convalescent home for a week it seemed much longer, but strangely I got used to the regime and at the end quite enjoyed being at the home. My parents came to collect me and it was a time of great joy and tears. The little girl who looked after me reported to them. I said goodbye to her and never saw her again. I forgot her name. But I still feel affection.

Illnesses were a regular occurrence of childhood. By the time I was five I had suffered and recovered from pneumonia, whooping cough and diphtheria. Later I was to contract mumps and then measles. Measles caused no end of a fuss. They put me into quarantine and inspected the school. But like Melchizedek, my measles proved to have no predecessor or successor. I was left with a limp for some months, the aftermath of the illness.

I spent three years at Morning Lane School, where the boredom of learning was interspersed with the joy of play and the interruption of illness. Then 1935 arrived and with it my seventh birthday. The time was at hand when I would have to leave for junior school.

7 The Question of My Estate

We sang hymns at assembly in Morning Lane School. 'Onward Christian Soldiers' with its rousing tune was a favourite but there was one I remember more vividly, 'All Things Bright and Beautiful'. This was not because of its first verse. Rather it was the second verse that intrigued me, with its strange imagery and social implications. It is no longer to be found in recent versions of the hymn. Like the third verse of 'God Save the Queen' it has been excised as if it never existed.

The verse ran in all its archaic splendour:

> The rich man in his castle,
> The poor man at his gate
> God made them high and lowly,
> And order'd their estate.

In my imagination I became that poor peasant. I stood at the broken-down gate of a tumbledown cottage crooked with age. My beard was long and white and I wore a white smock. I looked up at a lofty, high-walled castle. There on the battlements was a knight in shining armour, legs astride, certain of his power, holding an angled lance bearing a broad pennant. Imperiously he surveyed the countryside – his countryside. God ordered his estate and he hadn't done too badly. I had second thoughts and decided that I would be the knight. Then, like Good King Wenceslas's page, I could carry flesh, wine and winter fuel to the poor peasant and feel good.

Miss Gough, the headmistress, explained the hymn. Hers was a strange interpretation. She told us that we all had our place in life and should be satisfied with our lot and accept it. I had a feeling that we children of Morning Lane School were being consigned to the cottage gate rather than the castle. No doubt Miss Gough thought it necessary to console us, for children of our background were not expected to ascend the ladder of life but rather be left holding it for others. I was made to feel second class and I was resentful of her placid assumptions. Her philosophy was not at all acceptable to me.

Life was rough in the playground. One day when bending over a water fountain I had my head thrust forcibly on to the tap. Several front teeth fell out. More frightening were the big boys of the senior school, for Morning

Lane housed a senior as well as an infant school; a curious arrangement which meant that after a period of going to a junior school I would one day return to Morning Lane Senior School.

My father had gone to that school just before the First World War. It was, he said, a very tough school where the headmaster, a Mr Packham, had to rule with a rod of iron. He beat discipline into the boys with a walking stick. He had to, said my father, otherwise they would have run riot. Father had a great admiration for Mr Packham. But he remained a rebel at heart, for he spoke with glee of the time when the boys responded with dumb insolence. At register they did not respond when their names were called. In class they refused to answer any questions. They did not talk to each other. An uncanny quietness settled on the school. The great Mr Packham, for once, was baffled.

From what I could see, the school had not changed and was still tough. I saw the boys of the senior school as uncouth and unkempt. Their clothes were shabby and ragged. They ran about as a disorderly mob shouting and pushing each other. I had no desire to graduate into that school, yet it was my obvious destiny. My future lot in life stared me in the face and I abhorred it. I felt trapped. Was there no escape? I became determined never to go to that unpleasant school. Never! Never! Never! But I felt a sinking in my heart. 'There are other kinds of school,' said my mother. My ears pricked up. 'What sort?' 'Grammar schools where those nice boys go. You remember.'

I remembered. It was at Bethnal Green that I had seen a group of older boys dressed neatly and alike with school caps and blazers. They were the boys of Parmiter's School. Yes, I would like to go there. 'How do you get to a school like that?' 'You have to get a scholarship. It's not easy.' Scholarship. The magic gateway to another world. 'Your Aunt Ethel got a scholarship, you know, but there wasn't the money for her to take it up.'

Aunt Ethel was Nan's quiet daughter, who nearly died from meningitis. 'She's different to the rest of us. She doesn't talk much,' said mother.

I fell into deep thought. So there was a way out for such as us. Henceforth the scholarship was to be my goal and thus was ambition born out of necessity. 'I don't know why the boy's worrying so,' said my father, 'that's years ahead. He's got to go to junior school first.'

'But we have to look ahead,' said my mother. Father nodded. 'I want him to get a better start in life than I had.' His father had sent him to work at fifteen as a bottle-washer and my father had remained ever resentful, liable to flush with anger at the memory of it. My fear was that I, too, would end up as a bottle-washer in some grubby factory. I am sure that such precocious thoughts never entered the minds of middle-class children of those days with their assured futures.

So it was that Mother took me along to see Miss Gough to discuss my scholarship prospects on the day I left Morning Lane Infant School, although I had only just passed my seventh birthday and the scholarship lay three years ahead.

We saw Miss Gough in her office. My mother asked what were my chances of gaining a scholarship? Miss Gough, grey-haired and studious, hedged her answer. Her task was to soothe the parents of this little working-class boy. In her heart she knew that I was a hopeless case. She tried to be as kind as she could, but she was frank. She explained that I was not the scholastic type, but that, perhaps, I would be good with my hands. The grammar school, she explained, was not for me. There was not even the slightest chance of my gaining a scholarship. We should put that out of our minds to avoid disappointment. Perhaps Alan might make the Central School if he worked harder. There he could learn shorthand, typing and secretarial work instead of carpentry and metalwork at the senior school.

Thus was my estate ordered at the age of seven. I left her office dismayed, with my vanity wounded and a determined fury in my heart. I would get a scholarship, whatever Miss Gough thought.

8 Silver Jubilee

Before I was seven I was a child within a child's world. I thought my own thoughts and played my own games. The world of adults was foreign to me. Only the thoughts of the scholarship disturbed this closed world. I never read newspapers, only comics and my beloved *William* books. I lived in the adventures of Mickey Mouse, Tiger Tim and Rupert.

The dream of childhood was fading in 1935, the first year that I remember as a year. I did not know then that the world I was awakening into was as unreal as the empire of my mind, for it was the year of the Silver Jubilee, a year of adult fantasy.

It was still the age of steam and coal, and George V was the last monarch of that age. He ruled an empire linked by steam ships and steam trains. And how right it was for the London and North Eastern Railway to celebrate his Silver Jubilee with a new gleaming locomotive, the sleek and shining *Silver Link*.

Those interwar days of the steam train meant specifically for me Liverpool Street station. It was always a special treat when I went there with my mother, on a rattling tram, to meet my father on his way home from work. Alighting from the tram at its Bishopsgate terminus, we would push through the busy crowds into a hazy fairytale world of dark and bright. There, amid the encircling gloom of a winter's evening, Liverpool Street station glowed rosy in the diffuse light of its steamy and sooty splendour. There the railway track lay well below street level and Victorian stairways and elevated gangways, fashioned of ornamental cast iron, spanned the station. From these lofty walkways I viewed the station, which lay spread out before me like a gigantic model railway. Down below, crowds of people scuttled about like busy ants in endless streams between trains and exits. But they were nothing to me, for my attention centred on a disorder of black steaming locomotives, lords of the domain.

There was no mistaking their primitive power, the authority of the deep tuba-like beat of their voices as they puffed out buntings of black gritty smoke and pure white steam. These coalesced as they twisted upwards to form a flimsy fan vaulting that appeared to support the soot-encrusted canopy of glass. Ah, how today's boys would enjoy it. What they have missed!

I stood there, by my mother, entranced by this wondrous chaotic scene. I peered through this sombre chequered paradise of white and black for a glimpse of my father. Then when I saw him trudging along the iron

A souvenir mug for the Silver Jubilee of George V. (*Author's collection*)

walkways I shouted with joy and ran down to greet him with an unselfconscious kiss. I was that young.

There was something warm and homely in the Liverpool Street station of those days. As we left I threw a lingering glance back at that now lost world of steam.

The *Silver Link* was dedicated to the twenty-five years of King George V's reign, and he and Queen Mary were the emblems of Empire. They possessed a dignity that set them apart from mere mortals. They were creatures of a different world – the lofty world of Royalty and Empire. Together they stood for stability, not subject to the law of mortals. But they were creatures of a dying age. This remote couple in their strange splendour brought to the uncertain age of the thirties the solid virtues of an imperial past. All felt secure when they were on the throne; they were as solid and as sure as the mighty steam locomotive.

My mother took me to Buckingham Palace on the day of the jubilee and we were among the crowds that thronged around seeking a glimpse of

A street party in
Hackney during
the 1935 Silver
Jubilee. *(LMA)*

passing majesty. I remember that day as one of unalloyed joy untarnished
by the doubtful future. Outside the palace, pressed against the tall railings,
we met a Canadian lady to whom the Empire was a golden state. Many
thought like that then and not only those of the British Isles. The Empire
was a reality in which we believed. We were simple folk in those days.
She gave me a pretty paper rose of red, white and blue, a gift half-forgotten

A souvenir of the Spithead Review, Silver Jubilee, 1935. *(HMSO)*

yet still remembered; a fragile thing of Empire which I kept for many years. Eventually it was lost, as these things are. I remember her, and her enthusiasm, but I do not remember the King and Queen passing by. Doubtless they did.

The poorer streets of the East End of London were bedecked with banners, bunting and flags. Houses were ablaze with coloured decorations; every house was an explosion of red, white and blue. Gaudy decorations rose from pavement to rooftop. Flimsy armorials adorned the dwellings of the disinherited. Flags poked out in profusion from every window; Union Jacks in plenty but there were others from every known country and a few unknown countries of the world. Shields bearing portraits of the King and Queen were fastened to walls and long brightly coloured banners hung down from the gutters. Windowsills were draped as if they were Victorian mantelpieces.

These bright garish colours of celebration overwhelmed the greyness of the streets and mean houses. In Stevens Avenue banners crisscrossed the narrow street bearing messages: 'God Save the King', 'Poor But Loyal' and 'Lousy But Loyal'. Down below there were feverish preparations for the jubilee tea. Men placed trestle tables the length of the streets and women covered them with white cloths. An army of helpers ran backwards and forwards from street doors to tables, burdened with tea urns, fairy cakes, swiss rolls and sandwiches. The streets hummed with the excited noise of anticipation.

But not Darnley Road. It was a middle-class road and middle-class roads remained bare of decorations and devoid of street parties. The vulgar display of patriotism was not for them. When I could not get into the Stevens Avenue tea party my mother became concerned lest I miss out on a jubilee tea. She bustled around and Nan was called in. Eventually I ended up in some strange street in Bow enjoying a tea party with boys and girls whom I had never seen before and would never see again. But it was fun and mother was happy.

In July the King reviewed the Fleet at Portsmouth in the antique steam yacht *Victoria and Albert*. Much was made of George V as a sailor king.

The jubilee inspired me to start collecting things. At school I was given a jubilee mug and at Sunday school a jubilee cup and saucer. These I housed in my museum case – an upturned fish tank – together with a silver shilling of William IV, in mint condition, that my father had given me. There was a special issue of jubilee stamps, which was the start of my stamp collection. When I look back I can see that my entire collection was devoted to the monarchy. Royalty suffused our lives.

9   Summer Holidays

Each August we took a holiday by the seaside, at Margate, Ramsgate or Southend-on-Sea. On this Father insisted, although he could not often afford to be with us. He made this sacrifice so that Mother and I could stretch our holiday to three weeks.

It would be untrue to say that I remember these summer holidays as idyllic with broad beaches rolling into the distance, glowing golden under the rays of a relentless sun perched in a stark blue sky. Far from it. I suppose the beaches of Southend were golden when the sun shone, and they were certainly broad, too broad at times, for when the tide went out I never succeeded in reaching the sea. I do not remember much of a shining sun. But I do remember a day when a relentless wind swept the open beach, whipping up the sand into my eyes and ears and chastising my exposed flesh. Then we raced for the shelters, thoughtfully provided by the municipal authorities for the preservation of their visitors. I cried with pain and asked my mother to take me home, pleading: 'I want my own kitchen!' No wonder. We stayed in lodgings and after breakfast were locked out in all weathers until the evening when the landlady let us back in. That was the custom in those days. My memory of those rooms is of the washstand complete with a large jug of water, a broad washbasin, a soap dish and a slop bucket, not to mention a chamberpot under the bed.

Our meals were simple, often taken at the Beehive café. My lunch there was always steak and kidney pudding followed by college pudding, both the same shape – a curved truncated cone that was, come to think of it, reminiscent of an old-fashioned beehive. Mother left a tip for the waitress once a week, on the theory that it seemed more that way rather than give a minute daily tip.

Once we went to a cafeteria. This was something new. You could see meals laid out before you and you then chose what you fancied. I thought it a great idea, so much better than a waitress coming along with a menu, which was just words. Mother chatted to a lady who told us that the idea had come from America.

There were no McDonald's in those days, but there was the perennial fish and chips and saveloy and pease pudding. Saveloy was a boiled seasoned pork sausage. Vendors sold it from stalls lit by naphtha flares at night. I was transported to a state of pleasurable bliss and glowed with delight.

With my parents at Margate in 1931, in a happy mood. *(Author's collection)*.

With bucket and spade at Margate, aged three, in 1931. Something has gone wrong: I am on the verge of tears. *(Author's collection)*

On the beach
with my mother.
*(Author's
collection)*

Once, at the behest of my cub master, I kept a diary. It is sparse and factual but the effort of recalling the events at the end of each day and writing them down etched this holiday on my memory. On the cover of the diary I wrote: 'A Wilson August 1935 Age 7'. Inside were the events from Monday 29 July to Monday 26 August 1935. Much of the time was spent on the beach, often with new friends that I had met on holiday. I made friends easily in the days of my childhood, before the trauma of the war enclosed me in a carapace of reserve. I see a typical entry from my diary dated Monday 29 July and headed 'Southend':

> My mother and I went to Thorpe Bay my three friends and I went in the water and played with my boats we then went to dinner then we built a castle with a very big Dyke to keep the water out. After tea we had a game of Beach Ball. after we went home and had supper and it was my bedtime.

I adopted a purposeful attitude towards the mysterious sea and attempted to tame it either by building dykes to stop it or by guiding it into channels that I had dug. I was always unsuccessful. The problem with

Southend-on-Sea was the tide. When the tide went out it went right out and the sea disappeared altogether, leaving long wide bands of sand and mud that stretched to the horizon. 'Where has the sea gone?' I mused. I was determined to solve the mystery. So one day when the tide was right out I forced my mother on an expedition to find the sea's edge. We trudged on and on, through the golden sand to the estuary mud. Still no sea. And we never found it. An objective as elusive as the rainbow's end. There is a brief entry in my diary on Saturday 3 August:

> to-Day We followed the tide out my mother and my friends and i collected some pretty Stones and Shells and saw a Dog swim after a Ball. We played on the Beach and went home

What else was there to do? When the sea returned there was great excitement. I wrote on Thursday 1 August:

A page from my diary of 1935, when I was seven. *(Author's collection)*

> today i got up early and went for a walk when we got to the sea the tide was coming in so my mother helped me dig a channel and the water ran into it. after diner my friends and i built a harbour and we had some good fun all the afternoon

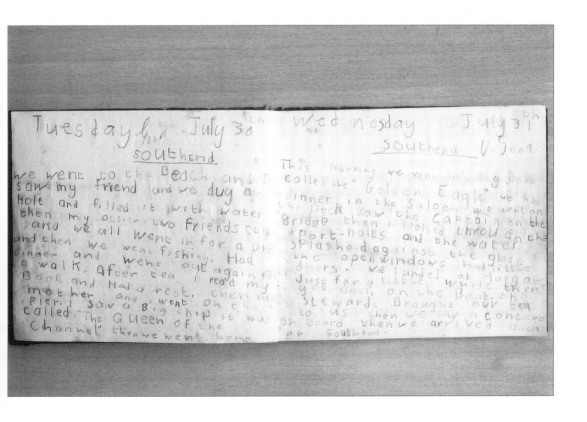

Sometimes the tide misbehaved, as it did on Wednesday 14 August:

> To-Day we had a picnic on the beach and had a game on the sands i
> made a model motor-boat with sand. The tide came in and the Big
> waves washed it away. We went into the Shelter and watched the tide
> come in and went home.

I still remember that event well and what I wrote was an
understatement of what happened, for on that afternoon there was a
strange incoming tide that caused great consternation. Most tides are
hesitant things that cannot make up their minds; they shillyshally about,
alternately advancing and retreating. There is comfort in their irregular
rhythms. That afternoon the tide was different. The sunbathers were
languid under the heat of a rare sun and picnickers leisurely sipped tea and
nibbled cakes. All was peace as the tide came in, the contemptuous
Southend tide shallow and without ripples. But this tide kept on coming in,
advancing relentlessly without ever once retreating. The sunbathers and
picnickers stared at it in amazement, transfixed by its purposeful advance.
They fell still and silent. Then suddenly, as the unexpected waters lapped
around them, there was pandemonium. Sunshades collapsed, tea things
sank and sandwiches floated away, to the delight of the gulls. The holiday-
makers – shouting, shrieking and squealing – retreated to the promenade,
their grey flannels and white dresses saturated with sea water, their thirties
synthetic sunbathing costumes ruined.

I looked at the wreck of this peaceful afternoon: upside-down sunshades
rotated slowly on the waves, clothing floated on the surface of the waters,
straw picnic baskets were shipwrecks emptied of all contents, and in
between was a scattering of ice-cream tubs, paper bags and bent straws.
This was the havoc wrought by the strange phenomenon of an aggressive
tide that did not wash to and fro with the expected rhythm; a tide to be
wary of. Now I see it as a strange allegory of the thirties.

One entry in my diary has the archaic flavour of 1935 about it. On
Sunday 4 August I wrote:

> We went to Shoeburyness and saw some bathing huts had tea at a
> farmhouse and we saw pups and the mother. and we fed the father at
> tea-time. We saw people in their tents and we rode home on a tram

Yes, there were still bathing huts for the gentle folk. We could not afford
one, so undressed discreetly under towels on the open beach.

The tram was one of the open double-deckers of that period. I remember
it so well with its charm. It was white and of the seaside, the upper deck
open to the blue sky. I clambered up the curling staircase to sit on the open

The Queen of the Channel was an object of my admiration in the 1930s. It was sunk during the gallant evacuation of troops from Dunkirk in 1940. *(Paddle Steamer Picture Gallery)*

top – heaven. There I inhaled the pungent smells of the sea. In the centre of the upper deck was a short pylon from which swung, at a low angle, a pole that picked up electricity from an overhead cable. This fascinated me and I would spend the journey in a state of timeless happiness watching the pole swing to-and-fro under a clear blue sky and an enchanting sun. That afternoon I felt the touch of paradise.

Southend pier was always an attraction. It was a long pier, the offspring of that tide and constructed so that ships could dock at low tide. On fine days we would walk its length to the very end and watch the men fishing. There were also other exciting happenings at the end of the pier. I wrote on Tuesday 30 July:

> After tea i read my Book and had a rest. then my mother and i went on the pier. i saw a Big ship it was called *The Queen of the Channel* then we went home.

To my young eyes the new *Queen of the Channel* was the most glamorous of ships – her hull was white and her twin funnels buff. I found out that the forward one was false, for she was a motor vessel. I saw her come in at night, ablaze with light from bow to stern. Lights were strung from her masts in a necklace of sparkling stars and the portholes gleamed like a multitude of luminous eyes. A hum of excited chatter came from her decks. The atmosphere was very lively. She was going to cross the Channel, which seemed to my young eyes the height of sophisticated travel, for on the other side they spoke French. In those simple times foreign lands had the aura of the court of the Caliph of Baghdad.

There was even more excitement for me on the next day, Wednesday 31 July:

> This morning we went on a Big Boat called the *Golden Eagle* we had dinner in the Saloon we went on Deck saw the Captain on the Bridge then i looked through the port-holes and the water splashed against the glass. the open windows had little doors. We landed at Margate just for a little while. then got back on the Boat. the Steward brought our tea to us then we saw a concert on Board then we arrived back at Southend.

The *Golden Eagle* was one of those pork-pie paddle steamers, so beloved of Londoners from early Victorian days. I find it difficult to believe that they have gone, for after the war they passed into history. My mother told me that the *Golden Eagle* was an old ship that had seen service in the Great War. I found it strange to associate this light-hearted old ship with war.

Southend pier – a favourite place. From it I saw the ill-fated *Queen of the Channel* and boarded the *Golden Eagle*. (*Author's collection*)

A poster advertising trips on the *Golden Eagle* in 1939. *(Paddle Steamer Picture Gallery)*

I see that all I recorded in my diary was tea-time (naturally) and the portholes (something new). I omitted more exciting events. For after I clambered on board I descended immediately to the engine room. Leaning over a gangway I peered through cloudlets of all-pervading steam to glimpse a rotating gleam of brass and steel that was the great reciprocating steam engine. I inhaled the tangy perfume of the pistons that sweated oil and steamy water. I admired the giant cylinders as they turned over slowly in their lazy strength. Eventually I was sated and so went back to the deck to witness the mighty paddles beat the water.

Nor did my diary record the alarming experience when the ship docked at Margate. A storm had come from nowhere and the swell of heavy seas rocked the paddle steamer to and fro. Suddenly, one giant paddle wheel rose out of the water and the deck tilted: a moment of danger. The ship was out of control with but one paddle in the water. The captain ordered all the passengers to move across the deck to counteract the tilt. It was all alarming but no one seemed afraid. Rather, we were all cross as the sea spray soaked us. Then the ship righted itself with a heave and one side of the ship scraped the dockside. 'He'll get in trouble for that,' said one critical passenger.

The old *Golden Eagle* has long gone, overtaken by progress, the steam-driven paddle no match for the jet aeroplane. Somehow I feel that if I wandered down to Tower Bridge today I would find the paddle steamers there, steam up, with crowds waiting at the quays and queuing at the ticket office for a trip to Southend, Margate and Ramsgate. Such is the persistence of the ghosts of the past.

I had an early interest in architecture, a love that has lasted all my life. So I persuaded my mother to take me about visiting churches, mills and castles. I see that I wrote on Monday 12 August:

after Dinner we went for a walk to [Great] StamBridge mills where they turn corn into flour. We saw Sutton church it is very old it was built in 1633. it is a very little church [the date on the porch door is 1633, but the church is thirteenth- and fifteenth-century and Norman]. We went home on a bus.

Again on Tuesday 20 August:

This morning i went to Little Wakering. We went into the church it was lit by oil lamps and was Built in 1425

I also detect some indication of a budding scientist with an insistence on numbers and dates. Monday 5 August was a Bank Holiday and we combined architecture with fun:

My mother and my friends and i went to the sports at Hadleigh Castle and saw Hadleigh Church and an Orchard We had milk on a house-Boat. We went home on a smart Bus

There is a photograph of me with new-found friends – alas, long forgotten – standing in front of a ruined castle, a castle famous as a subject of a painting by Constable. It was as ruinous then as it was in 1935. Far below is a railway line and beyond the sea.

As for the houseboats, they were still to be found in those days – homes for the poor – moored along the river. Some offered refreshments. The smart bus that caught my eye must have been one of the new streamlined coaches that appeared in the thirties, replacing the angular charabancs.

The church of St Mary the Virgin, Little Wakering. I had an early interest in churches. *(Author's collection)*

Another attraction of Southend that fascinated me was the carnival. I wrote on Wednesday 21 August:

> In the afternoon we saw the Carnival Procession there were some Big heads and King Carnival. We got on a tram and went home.

Rain was forever a problem at Southend. I wrote on Friday 23 August:

> This morning it was raining and we went into the Shelter till it stopped then it started again we got under the umbrella.

The attraction of Southend on a rainy day was the Kursaal. It was the local gambling den, full of pin machines. Once I made all of 1s 11d after I found a defective machine that returned the steel ball whether I won or lost, and when I won it gave me money as well. I was on to a good thing. But eventually some keen-eyed attendant spotted me and repaired the machine.

With friends I made in 1937, standing before Hadleigh Castle. The tug-of-war is yet to come. (Author's collection)

There were other machines, some containing alluring prizes, all protected by glass casings. In some there were grab cranes that opened their jaws as they descended on a prize. But the prizes were of glass or shining metal that easily slipped through their grasp, and when on rare occasions success seemed assured the grab would unaccountably release its gift. It was so unfair. 'You don't stand a chance,' said a man. 'They fix it like that.' All that ever could be won were cylindrical sweets, unique to this machine.

More promising than these cranes were rotating circular tables, invitingly loaded with bottles of cheap perfume, glass ashtrays, plastic boxes and the like. These prizes were pushed towards the rim by a metal arm. With any luck they could be guided down a chute. Uncle Fred, who visited us with Nan and Granddad for the day, was an expert. For an hour or two he would practise, losing sixpence after sixpence, but once his hand was in he won a crop of prizes.

Alas, all good things come to an end, and Southend-on-Sea *was* good despite the inclemency of the weather. The sad end is marked in my diary entry of Saturday 24 August, headed ominously 'Hackney' and not 'Southend':

> we went shopping to-day and after Dinner we took the luggage to the station and then went to the Beach. we went Back to the Station at five to catch our train we had a nice ride home and we arrived at eight o'clock.

I did not record my tears on returning to Hackney. But I often cried when I returned to the grey city and its dreary pall of smoke, a depressing contrast to the lively seas and skies of the seaside. The next day I wrote:

> This morning i went to see my Gran and had a Dinner with her. I went to Sunday school and had some Boys home to tea and we had a Game of cowBoys and soldiers and played with my Dog i went to my friend's house until it was time to go home.

Normal life had resumed. Sunday dinner at Gran's. The boredom of Sunday school. I wrote on Monday 26 August:

> my friend called for me This morning with his Dog and i took my Dog and we went to the Common and had a good Game we went home to tea and saw my nan.

To see Nan on a Monday at 12 Darnley Road was a break with routine. No doubt it made up for the usual Saturday afternoon visit which we missed because of our holiday.

Looking back I can see how cosy holidays were at Southend. There would be visits from Father, at the weekend, and from Nan and uncles and aunts during the week. Southend was a home from home, an extension of the East End of London.

I see that I did not record our visit to the military airfield at Rochford where I saw rows of brightly coloured biplanes lined up on a green field. I now know that these were Hawker Furys and that Rochford airfield was to suffer during the Battle of Britain. So even in the carefree days of childhood, when all about me seemed serene and peaceful, there lurked the omens of war to come. Even those pleasure boats, the *Queen of the Channel* and the *Golden Eagle*, were sailing into a grim future. Of this I was blissfully unaware. I had no inkling that once more the *Golden Eagle* was to go to war. She would evacuate children from London in September 1939 and would face German dive bombers at Dunkirk. She proved a lucky ship and survived the ordeal of Dunkirk, unlike her more modern sister ship the *Crested Eagle*.

The *Queen of the Channel*, now forgotten, should be remembered in the annals of history for she was a ship of salvation. The scene is different from that of the pier at Southend. It is another time and another place: the immortal East Mole of Dunkirk. Instead of happy holiday-makers there are desperate troops in battle khaki being dive-bombed on the beaches.

The *Golden Eagle*. We once boarded this ship at Southend for a return trip to Ramsgate. *(Paddle Steamer Picture Gallery)*

The *Golden Eagle* with evacuees at Gravesend, September 1939. *(Paddle Steamer Picture Gallery. Source and permission from John Mason)*

The evacuation of troops from Dunkirk is going badly. Rowing troops from the beaches to distant ships is proving too slow. The expectation of Churchill and his generals is that the bulk of the British Army will be captured. A Captain Tennant is standing on the East Mole. He decides on a new scheme. But can it be done? 'We'll try it,' he announces. 'Signal the nearest ship to come in.' The *Queen of the Channel* is the nearest ship and she responds. Can she be secured against the Mole? She noses against it, the bow is fastened and the stern swings against the Mole. Somehow she is docked and soon men climb aboard and Captain Tennant sighs with relief. It can be done! She pulls away. Alas, a Stuka puts a bomb through her deck and the *Queen of the Channel* flounders, but she has shown the way. Other ships follow and the East Mole becomes the sacred way of the British Army. The Army is saved.

But all that horror was still five years ahead; for the present we languished in the balmy days of peace.

10   Death of a King

O n a bleak January night in 1936 the old King died. It was an unforgettable night, engraved on my memory. I remember exactly where I was at the time – right at the bottom of the lower staircase in 12 Darnley Road.

The crisis had broken down the barriers between us Wilsons in the basement and the Hubbles upstairs. Now the unused lower staircase between our basement and the upper house became the stage for a drama about to unfold.

I recall the scene as if it were a waxwork tableau. I was standing at the foot of the stairs with Mother. Father was half-way up and, at the top, bending over the banisters, was Mrs Hubble, so like Queen Mary in carriage and appearance. Hidden in the depths of his study, Mr Hubble was stationed by a wireless set and repeated the news to Mrs Hubble, who relayed it down to us. In this way, scattered up and down the stairs, we learnt of the sad and momentous event as the oft-quoted phrase, 'the King's life is moving peacefully to its close', floated down.

I was impressed by the dignified and decorous manner of the King's departure. He was born of an age of certainty and was dying to a stately timetable, the end as neat as a play by Terence Rattigan, all shipshape for the Sailor King. But I found it strange that death was so predictable and so ordered. Is death like this? Do you die to a timetable? Is death this quiet and this peaceful?

Today we know differently. Some have alleged that the King's physician, Lord Dawson of Penn, injected a lethal dose of morphine so that the King would die in time for the morning press. It was considered that the morning papers would give a more dignified report of his death than the racy evening press, hence the ditty that was current at the time, although I did not hear it until much later:

> Lord Dawson of Penn
> Has killed lots of men.
> So that's why we sing
> God save the King.

Dignity was the order of the day, and after the well-ordered death came a sombre lying in state. The night before the funeral his four sons stood on duty, like medieval princes, around the catafalque. There was, however, a discordant note, for during the funeral procession, as the gun carriage bearing the King's body jogged along, the imperial crown on the coffin broke apart, and the great Maltese cross of sapphires and diamonds that surmounted the crown fell into the gutter.

The passing of King George V saw the passing of an era. I had known no other king in my short life. I had thought of him as one of the immortals – the Empire incarnate. He was the emblem of Empire; a naval person who personified the power of the sea that held the Empire together. While he lived we bathed in a world of Victorian certainty and the Empire was safe.

But death comes to us all and it had come to him, as it was later to come to his Empire. He was succeeded by a child of the times: King Edward VIII. Gone was the majesty that girds a King. Instead there was a playboy, a Mr 1930s, a King who had uttered when he saw the fall of the crown: 'Christ! What will happen next?' We were all to find out in the coming months and in the coming years the answers to that question.

Peace was fading. In March Hitler moved into the Rhineland. The black-and-white newsreels of those days showed the steel-helmeted Germans parading through the streets of Rhineland villages, cheered by flag-waving crowds. A small boy knows little of the politics of things but he recognises what is ominous, and I felt a shiver of cold fear as I saw the jackboots marching in triumph. It was the beginning of the end of my age of innocence. I was just eight and the problems of the world were forcing their way into my life. I was to find that our lives are but corks bobbing on a turbulent ocean of events, and such little direction as we can impart to our lives is overwhelmed by the relentless beating of the restless waves.

Lolling comfortably in a plush seat of the Pavilion cinema with my mother, I watched a newsreel intently. I saw a bull-headed man, hair cropped to the skin, ranting in a strange language, gesticulating theatrically from a balcony at a chanting crowd below. His bombastic performance exuded a raw and ominous power evoking both fear and mirth. His was the dusky image of a Mars. This Mars was Mussolini, puffed up with power, making war on Abyssinia. The newsreel cut to a shot of Italian bombers droning over a barren rocky landscape, with canisters falling from them. Cut to a few huddled bodies in tattered and acid-eaten rags, dead and dying Abyssinian peasants, drenched with mustard gas. 'What a terrible death,' Nan was to say at Beale Place one Saturday afternoon. After the newsreel ended the mighty Wurlitzer organ emerged from the depths, like Britannia rising above the waves, roaring music, its illuminated panels changing colour like a demented chameleon. A stream of popular music flooded out, 'I get a kick out of you' and 'Isn't this a lovely day', while I ate an ice-cream and waited for the main feature.

11   Orchard School

I should have gone to the Berger Road Junior School, by the paint factory, but this was considered a rough school and my parents pushed hard to get me to The Orchard. The Orchard had a better academic record and was new, not at all forbidding but light and airy. I had escaped from Victorian gloom. The school had moved from Orchard Street, and in the move, had taken the opportunity to drop 'street' from its name. It thus broke away from the usual unimaginative practice of naming a school after the nearest road, lane or street. It was not all advantage, for although its name sounded, shall we say, up-market or 'posh', at sports meetings the two syllables did not lend themselves to an encouraging chant. The thin up-and-down piping of 'OR-CHARD, OR-CHARD' could not compete with the heavy throaty beat of 'BER-GER-ROAD, BER-GER-ROAD'.

With fellow pupils at Orchard School just before Christmas 1935. I have seized the rocking horse after a struggle. I was very pushy in those days. Despite the photograph it was not a mixed school. The boys and girls occupied separate halves of the school and playground. Holding the board is the girl, born on the same day as me, whom I admired from a distance and wished to marry. (*Author's collection*)

In those days, even in the junior schools, the sexes were segregated. Although Orchard took in both boys and girls, a high wall separated our playgrounds and we were taught in separate classes. From that time onwards I lost contact with girls. By the time I was ten they had become as remote as creatures from another planet – indeed, they became as strange as Martians. Only at rare times did the sexes mingle. One was when we sat the scholarship and I remember gazing at one pretty girl who had been born on exactly the same day as myself – Rosemary. Towards her I had romantic longings. It is surprising that vague imaginings of love and marriage exist in the young child before sexual maturity. I dreamed of marrying her one day, but it was ever love at a distance. I knew of her because our mothers knew each other, but we never even spoke.

None of my friends at Morning Lane School came with me to Orchard. Most went to Berger Road School, and in the future I was only to see them at St Luke's Church or meet them in the street when we ganged up. I arrived at Orchard in the autumn – the conker season. Horse chestnuts were falling from the trees in the parks and commons and boys were out collecting them. Then, on the asphalt playground of the Orchard School, we took part in the game of conkers. To play, a horse chestnut was pierced and a short piece of string threaded through the hole and knotted. The conker was now ready for combat.

The game was a duel. One boy would hold his conker dangling down on the end of a string while the other swung his at it, like a mace and chain. Boys took alternate turns. The duel ended when one conker broke up under the onslaught. The winning conker added to any value it had, one for winning plus the value of the defeated conker.

I was never successful at this game. I would watch aghast as my favourite conker slowly decomposed under the blows of my opponent's. First, the shell would crack and fall away. Then the soft centre would crack and split and finally fall into small pieces. At first I was naïve, but then I noticed that other boys with an ingenious turn of mind devised various forms of conker pre-treatment, which hardened soft conkers into stone. Toughening conkers was the subject of much talk. I went around gaining the secrets of conker reinforcement from other boys. Some boys favoured baking, while others pickled them in vinegar. I never discovered the best treatment for, whatever I did, my conkers always failed in contest.

Herbert Morgan, a sparse cockney boy, prepared the impregnable conker. Like him it was small, hard and wizened. All conkers, green, baked, pickled or otherwise, broke against it. Each day we would meet in the playground to watch it register yet another triumph. Because of its high conker value there was no shortage of challengers and we queued for the privilege of having our conkers smashed. But the day of nemesis came, as it always does. A gangling boy challenged with the softest of soft conkers. Herbert

Morgan swung the stone-hard conker down, hit the soft conker and broke up. We were all amazed – I suppose some sort of stress fatigue had at last caught up with the old conker.

Marbles was the other game of the playground. In the simple game a pair of marbles was placed on the ground and the opponent would attempt to hit them by rolling a marble at them. If he missed, the marble was lost. If he hit, then he won the pair. Some boys would place a single marble on a ridged manhole cover and offer five if it were hit. This was a winning strategy, except when I tried it. Freddie Marshall constructed an elaborate machine out of a shoebox, with holes and chutes and all sorts of interesting runways. It was something of which Heath Robinson would have been proud. I planned similar devices in my mind but never got round to making them.

Orchard School was a new building in the 1930s, light and airy, almost Arts and Crafts, in contrast to gloomy Victorian schools. *(LMA)*

I found that at Orchard I had, mercifully, left slates behind me, but here I was to meet another fiendish grown-up device – pen and ink. These were the days before ballpoints – one of the greatest inventions of the human mind – and although fountain pens were known they were not allowed or affordable. Ink was contained in china inkwells, which were set into our wood and cast-iron desks. Stained desktops told of the struggles of generations of boys to master the art of pen and ink, and inkwells stuffed with blotting paper told of their rebellion against it. Broken nibs, with their two jagged edges, were stuck in desktops, walls and blackboards.

How I wished for my pencils as I scratched away with steel, ink-laden nib. Ink flew about in all directions, staining my clothes and landing as blots on the pages of my exercise book. Characters written down lost their form as I smudged them into illegibility and my arms became stained blue-black. My arithmetic declined, not because I lacked a grasp of the subject but rather from my failure to read my own characters.

My learning remained mediocre. In my first term at Orchard I was sixteenth out of thirty-nine in a not very bright class. All told, my early years at Orchard were summed up in one report: 'Alan could do much better work if he paid more attention.' So much for ambition and constancy of purpose. My scholastic performance varied considerably over the years, depending, it seemed, on my relationship with the teacher: improving with sympathy and declining with antipathy.

Lessons were boring and gave me no joy. The most tedious were those on arithmetic. Apart from the awkward vulgar fractions, we had to factorise numbers, find the highest common factor (HCF) and the lowest common multiple (LCM), for what use I never understood. And in those days before decimal currency, teachers took sadistic pleasure in making us convert sums like £4 5s 6¼d into decimals. As there were 20 shillings to the pound, this part was easy, but pennies, at 240 to the pound, were a problem in an age without computers.

Now that they have gone, I look back on our old imperial units with affection: those illogical hundredweights and stones; those bushels and pecks; those rods, perches and poles; those pounds, shillings and pence, not forgetting the humble farthing. The farthing was a diminutive quarter of the old penny, and with one of these my mother, as a child, could buy a bag of sweets. Those were bright Edwardian days when a pound meant a golden sovereign and not a piece of brass. Those imperial units were symbols of an equally illogical Empire that splashed broad patches of red across the globe. The Empire has gone now, together with golden sovereigns and silver threepenny bits.

Sad thoughts, but back to the dullness of school. The other subjects were almost as tedious as arithmetic. But amid the gloom of grey, tiresome lessons that discouraged learning there appeared a chink of light, small but

LONDON COUNTY COUNCIL

Nov. 1935 — Apr. 1936

THE ORCHARD L.C.C. (J.B.) SCHOOL School

Report on Attendance, Conduct and Progress, for the Elementary School Year ended

Name *Wilson Alan.*   No. of Pupils in Class: *39*

Class or Standard *2b*.   Attendance *V. G.*   Place in Class: *16*

Note—Ex.: Excellent; V.G.: Very Good; G.: Good; V.F.: Very Fair; F.: Fair.

Religious Knowledge *G*.   Handwriting *F*.   Additional Subjects

Reading *V. G.*   Arithmetic *V. F.*

Spelling *G*.   Science *V. F.*   *Recitation G.*

Composition *F. G*.   Drawing *F. G*.

Practical Work *G*.   Geography *F. G*.

Needlework   History *F. G*.

CONDUCT: *Very fair.*

REMARKS: *Alan could do much better work if he paid more attention*

Parent's Signature. *Y. A. Wilson*   Class Mistress. *K.S.J.*

Form E/I — 9

500,000—(21B) 28/11/33.

Head Master / Head Mistress.

My 1936 Orchard
School report.
*(Author's
collection)*

stimulating, that lit in me the desire for scholarship. I can still remember
those lessons today and they remain in my mind as a coherent whole. They
were not part of the routine of learning but occasional talks given by the
headmaster, Mr Verrier. The subject he made live was, of all subjects,
ancient history, but Mr Verrier was an inspirational teacher. He told us of
the origins of civilisation, a subject that has never ceased to grip me.
I learnt that once the world was different and was a world where none of
the everyday things around me existed. That once man had been like the

animals and, to survive, hunted game on the sparse savannah and gathered fruits, berries and nuts from the woods. That once mankind's only tools were of rough fractured stone and that even the simple wheel awaited invention. Then something marvellous happened: civilisation.

Civilisation, so Mr Verrier told us, had dawned in the land of the two rivers, Mesopotamia, which lay between the Euphrates and the Tigris. More spectacular was another that arose along the River Nile. There has been much argument as to what civilisation is, but to me it was manifest by the giant pyramids at Giza, that inscrutable sphinx and those strange Egyptian gods with bodies of men and heads of beasts. I also learnt of war: of the centuries of conflict between the Babylonians, Assyrians and Egyptians and the triumph of the Persians and their Empire.

I remember little science being taught at school. My idea of science came from Mother taking me to the Exhibition Road museums. First, we would go to the Natural History Museum to see the giant whale and the dinosaurs. But my favourite was the Science Museum because it was a hands-on museum with working models that children could activate.

At Orchard I started violin lessons. It had nothing to do with my love of music and everything to do with avoiding the senior school. If I failed the scholarship, as seemed more than likely, then there was still the chance of avoiding the dreaded senior school by going to a central school. These schools taught subjects such as shorthand, typing and office work. The headmaster of the local central school was known to love music and had formed a school orchestra. At any interview it would clearly help to show an interest in the subject, hence my violin lessons at 6*d* a lesson. It was a waste of hard-earned money. Besides having no aptitude for the violin, I was disinclined to practise. The violin bored me. After a year or so it was clear I was going nowhere. My music master, who was German, could stand it no longer and one day he said to me, 'Vilson, Vilson, if you practise for a million years you will never learn to play the violin.' I felt somewhat discouraged, as a million years seemed rather a long time to wait for uncertain success. Sammy, who was a very poor scholar, played the violin well. Once I watched him perform before the whole school, surprised, perhaps, that he was chosen. Then, as he started playing, his silly-looking podgy face was transformed. Entranced by his own music he gave himself up to it completely and a divine look of ethereal bliss suffused his countenance. Then I knew that I was missing something that I would never possess.

I remember little of sport except swimming, which was Mr Verrier's favourite and the one sport for which I showed some aptitude. At first I had struggled to learn, for I found the breaststroke, which father tried to teach me, too complicated. Then I watched Billy the dog swim. He managed

L.FRANKS   E.MUSGROVE R.SMULEVITCH   R.GREGORY   R.P.HALL   A.D.WILSON   R.BROWNING
L.JAMES K.KEISLER   H.SABNER   W.A.SMITH   J.LITTLE   J.HICKSON   W.SUMSION   J.KENSBY   R.MARTINEAU

S.FREEDMAN   J.JONES   G.HOTTEN   R.WALLER
C.JOHNSON   J.PHILLIPS   C.LOGAN   K.LOVELL   J.ROGERS

easily enough, so I copied his uncomplicated doggy paddle. It worked and eventually I upgraded it to a kind of crawl.

And so the years at Orchard passed contentedly enough, with such small events rippling the waters of life. My schooling continued on its erratic course and I languished behind the leading lights, Phillips and Susman, and the also-rans, Rosner and Hall. The moment of truth – the scholarship examination – grew ever closer, and over all hung the ominous clouds of an approaching war.

The swimmers of Orchard School, 1938. I am second from the right in the top row. Note how ill-fed some of the children are. (*Author's collection*)

12 Empire

T he headmaster strode in short sharp strides to the dais. His presence was commanding, his demeanour and stature Napoleonic. His eyes swept the hall once, and once only; clear blue eyes that pierced us to the very soul. He might have been the French emperor before Austerlitz. Instead, he was Mr Verrier on Empire Day and just as formidable. Both were imperial occasions.

There were two days that stood out in the school year: one was Empire Day – 24 May – and the other Armistice Day, in those days always remembered on 11 November. We were told that the eleventh hour of the eleventh day of the eleventh month was when the Great War had ended. That day we would all stand in the hall and wait for 11 a.m. to strike, when a silence was observed for those who had died.

This silence could be heard, a positive thing that came suddenly on the hour as all the sounds of the city faded: the clatter of the horses, the hooting of the motor vehicles, the street cries and the hum and buzz of general noise. The silence lasted two minutes and seemed like two hours. It was a solemn and memorable occasion. In these realistic and practical days we do not allow the wheels of commerce and industry to be so interrupted, not even for two minutes, and we put off remembrance to the nearest Sunday. So convenient.

Empire Day, the anniversary of Queen Victoria's birthday, was the complement of Armistice Day. Both glorified the Empire in their different ways. While Armistice was the day of sad victorious war, Empire Day was that of triumphant peace. On Empire Day the headmaster would assemble the school and talk to us about imperial glories. He would wave at a large wall map of the world that hung behind the stage, showing the Empire sprawled crimson across the world, encircling the globe like a ragged shawl. Its extent impressed us all. The headmaster would tell us with pride that it was the greatest Empire that the world had ever seen and occupied a quarter of the world's surface, an Empire on which the sun never set. The headmaster would talk about the many peoples of the Empire, of the many races who comprised a fifth of the world's population.

So it was that the Empire became a living thing to me, as it was to all children. None could doubt its power. That this Empire was overblown and overextended never occurred to me. It was, in reality, like a taut balloon that would burst asunder at the slightest prick. The Empire had glamour, with its noble knights and heroines who upheld its honour on land, sea and air. Year after year the flamboyant Sir Malcolm Campbell, in his *Bluebirds*, raised the world's land speed record to keep it safely in the Empire. He was a hero to us schoolboys, his every success whispered from boy to boy. Miss Amy Johnson was the Empire's heroine. The newsreels showed her, in flying jacket and helmet, leaning against the open cockpit of her fragile biplane. She had flown from England to Australia along the route Croydon–Baghdad–Karachi–Rangoon–Singapore–Darwin, all fiefs of the Empire. This in the days when to fly in an aeroplane from London to Paris was an adventure. Her flight took her across land and sea, over mountains and above jungle and desert – all the varied terrains of an Empire of which she was an embodiment, as surely as Drake. All this was done, the poster assured us, on Summer Shell. This was the Empire before the fall, before it was to become, in the words of Kipling, at one with Nineveh and Tyre.

Today we regard all this sort of thing as anachronistic and reactionary, as indeed it was, but then it was different and it made us boys happy in our poverty to belong to such a great Empire. We joined in with gusto when we sang:

Some talk of Alexander, and some of Hercules;
Of Hector and Lysander, and such great names as these;
But none of the world's brave heroes, there's none that can compare
With a tow, row, row, row, row, row, for the British Grenadier.

I knew who Alexander was, but who were Hector and Lysander?

I remember a vast painting hanging beside the map. It was of a ship steaming under a clear blue sky on the straight and pure blue waters of the Suez Canal – port out, starboard home. The deck was festooned with a scattered array of daffodil-shaped ventilator ducts, yellow under a glaring sun, while white-clad members of the Raj lounged on the rails. It was a symbol of Empire, serene and confident. I have remembered this timeless painting over the years, perhaps because I unconsciously recognised that which I now consciously know: that it symbolised our maritime empire. This canal was the central part of a long blue highway to the Indian Raj, the heart of the Empire, a heart far from its head.

Beside the sunny painting of the Suez Canal was a sombre black-and-white lithograph. The scene was ominous. A grey battleship was ploughing through dark, stormy seas; evil seas disturbed by a forest of erupting tall geysers. They puzzled me, these falling towers of water. What were these sinister waterspouts? I had never seen anything like them. Later, I found out that they were caused by plunging shells. In the foreground, on the steel deck of an armoured ship, stood a lone boy, dying. Underneath the lithograph I read the legend: 'Jack Cornwell VC'. He had died at the Battle of Jutland. He was of the lower orders, he knew his place, it was the bloody deck of a shattered battleship and he had died there. Such was the price of Empire.

Our headmaster was far from being an unthinking jingoist; he had the feel of history and the rise and fall of empires. Thus it was one Empire Day that he shattered my illusions when he told the school that we should talk of the Commonwealth rather than Empire, that all the peoples of the Empire were equal and that we in Britain were not the masters but should be the friends of the other peoples of the Commonwealth. I did not like this idea at all. I could not bear the idea of sharing our Empire out. It seemed an abdication from Empire. Even as a boy I realised that these modern liberal ideas were but the first faint soundings of the drum of long retreat. I was disturbed. All was not well. Our Empire was not all great.

Once a term the headmaster would take a class in the main hall, when he would talk on his subject, ancient history, and the first empires of mankind. So absorbing were his talks that I still remember them. Indeed, they are the only lessons I remember from my childhood. They instilled in me a love of that period of history that saw the creation of civilisation. The headmaster talked with passion of the land of the two rivers, of Ur of Chaldees and of the long rivalry between Babylon and Nineveh; of Hammurabi, the first law-giver, and his city of the hanging gardens. He talked of Egypt, of the long river of the Nile and the pyramid of Cheops. From him I learnt that empires came and passed away. That they rose from the dust, grew into eminence and then crumbled into ashes. I remembered the headmaster's chart of history. It was a long wall chart, 3 feet high, running the full length of the main corridor and showing the history of civilisation, illustrated with scenes of war and peace, art and everyday life.

Each day as I shuffled slowly in the queue for assembly I had ample time to study the course of history from Sumer and Egypt to the present day. The scenes unfolded: the Egyptians building the pyramids, the Romans storming a castle sheltering under their testudos of shields, Christopher Columbus confronting the natives of America, and Nelson dying in Hardy's arms at Trafalgar.

More absorbing for me was the depiction of the rise and fall of empires. Bands of colour ran horizontally along the chart under the pictures, representing the leading powers of the day. On the left, at the start of civilised history, were two coloured bands, a yellow one for ancient Egypt and a blue one for Sumer, the land of the pyramid and the land of the ziggurat. As history unfolded from left to right these bands narrowed and finally disappeared. The red band of Assyria suddenly appeared and displaced all others as that warlike country conquered the world. Then it was cut off as sharply as it came when Nineveh fell, and the colours of the

Chaldean and Medean empires appeared. In turn these were displaced by the single green band of the Persian Empire. It, too, vanished as Alexander and then Rome conquered the world. The finale disappointed me. I had expected to see a single red band for a dominant British Empire. But instead there was a rainbow of bands and Britain was only one of many, sharing honours with the USA, Germany, France, Japan and Russia. This was all at variance with the concept of empire that had been foisted on me. The dream was tainted. The Empire was, indeed, a Commonwealth. Then I remembered at assembly the headmaster would on occasion read the *Recessional* of Kipling:

> God of our fathers, known of old
> Lord of our far-flung battleline,
> Beneath whose awful hand we hold
> Dominion over palm and pine
> Lord God of Hosts, be with us yet.
> Lest we forget – lest we forget!
> Lo all our pomp of yesterday
> Is one with Nineveh and Tyre

And so it proved. Once the highway of Empire stretched like a ruby necklace around the world; dotted with glistening jewels from England to India: Gibraltar, Malta, Suez and Aden. A long pendant dangled south from Cairo to the Cape. But the time was to come when the jewels loosened and were lost forever. Now the Empire has gone. Gone so utterly that but a few tiny rubies speck the atlas of the world. Gone so completely that we have surrendered.

Our currency, the proud illogical currency of Empire, pounds, shillings and pence, is no more. Gone are the humble farthing, four to the old penny, the agreeable tanner and the loved threepenny piece. What a fuss there was in 1937 when the minute silver threepenny piece was replaced by a twelve-sided coin. Once there were twelve pennies to the shilling and twenty shillings to the pound. Now there is no shilling. Gone too are that illogical pair, the florin and the half-crown. There remains in splendid memory the king of our currency, the white-and-black £5 note, large and crisp, the plain but majestic note of Empire.

God bless it. God bless them all. All gone.

RIP £ s d.

13   A New Church Hall

In those days, outside the family, the centre of social life was the church; the Church of England, with its Sunday school, Mothers' Union, Men's Club, scouts and Guides. I joined the cubs and my mother the Mothers' Union. Father was a scout master and a leading light, if that is the word, in the dreaded Men's Club.

St Luke's was a solid Victorian Gothic church with a stone spire. It did not soar but was firmly rooted in the ground. So recent was its foundation that Granny Wilson had known all its vicars. Granny no longer attended as she had fallen out with the Mothers' Union because of the C. of E.'s habit of backbiting, a common woe in that organisation. Instead she made do with services on the wireless and a view of the church spire that could just be seen across the rooftops.

Opposite the church lay the Woodbine Cottages, a remnant and reminder of a more remote past when Hackney was a village. Again opposite the church, but further on, was the centre of St Luke's lively social life, the new church hall, or the New Institute as it was called. It essayed the Scandinavian civic style of the thirties and sported a small cupola. Its foundation stone bore the inscription: 'To the Glory of God and in thanksgiving for the erection of this Church Hall, this tablet was unveiled by the Bishop of London November 2nd 1935.'

Between church and New Institute lay an unmade square, a much-frequented tryst for teenage boys and girls who, after church, would gather there in aimless packs, lounging against walls and engaging in apparently desultory chat. Some things never change.

Once there had been an Old Institute off Morning Lane where, in the late eighteenth century, Priestley, the discoverer of oxygen, had preached. Now it was decrepit. The interior was a galleried hall, dark, dusty and shabby but much loved. Small children loved it for its nooks and crannies, and the many small rooms that led off the dim U-shaped gallery which ran round three walls of the hall and made ideal hiding places for a game of hide-and-seek. It was a mysterious and wonderful place for small children to play in, unfettered by the prohibition of church elders, for the Old Institute was so old and battered that children could batter it no more. In the gloom of a cold winter's afternoon, we cubs would gather round the friendly tortoise stove with its red-hot glowing coals and listen to the adventures of Mowgli in the dim light. We all felt at home.

The days of the Old Institute were numbered with the coming of the new vicar. Mr Anton had the appearance and suave manner of George Sanders, a well-known actor of the time. He was a man of some dignity. Mr Anton looked at the beloved Old Institute and saw it as it was and not as we imagined it. He decreed that the time had come for a bright, new Institute. A plot of wasteland opposite the church was acquired.

A frenzied fund-raising campaign was launched, where every aspect of church life was subordinated to the quest for money. Staid middle-class ladies, the beautiful but delicate Mrs Bonifin, the earnest Miss Collins and even the haughty wife of the vicar hawked bricks for the New Institute for a shilling a time. Included in the price was the right to sign one's name in pencil on the brick, thus acquiring a sort of immortality, albeit a hidden one. Once I did like to think that somewhere, deep in the foundations, lay a brick with my name on it.

St Luke's Church, Hackney, and the New Institute (photographed in 1995, but now demolished). *(Author's collection)*

To me the New Institute was a building destitute of warmth. It was clean, it was neat, it was well planned, but oh so cold. It lacked the essential patina of age. The walls were painted in chilling yellow and the stairways were of harsh concrete with banisters of black-painted iron. I never felt comfortable in it. It was ambitious and unusual, an upside-down building where the main hall was on the first floor, supported by a plethora of small rooms below. It was cheaper to build it that way. Money was short and the New Institute ended up smaller than intended, so that dressing-rooms for the stage were cramped; but money was found for the cupola which adorned an otherwise plain structure.

A chorus of complaints greeted its completion. It was too small. The dressing-rooms were inadequate. Why was the hall on the first floor? And why was money wasted on the cupola? And the caretaker's flat was only suitable for midgets, yet in the war it was to serve as the vicarage. Despite all this, an impartial observer would have to admit that for a church hall it was a grand affair, and escaped the vernacular style so common then.

There were other grumbles. In the thirties ballroom dancing was a universal craze, so the main hall had been purpose-built with a maple dance floor so that it could be hired out for dancing. Funds were needed, for even after completion of the hall many bills remained to be paid. It would be pennies from heaven. Paying customers were given priority and church organisations found that the main hall was not available on Saturday nights, when it was filled with strangers who danced to the swinging sounds of the thirties. One Saturday night curiosity got the better of me and I went to see the couples dancing to the syrupy beat of a swing band. I was soon spotted and thrown out. I glowered with resentment. It was our institute! Not theirs! I had paid a shilling for my brick! I owned part of it! I had a right! It hadn't happened in the days of the Old Institute. There were many sighs for that, but then who wanted to dance in the Old Institute?

The cubs and scouts were dissatisfied. The dance floor was too slippery for their games and they too lamented the loss of the Old Institute. In turn the vicar frowned on their activities, which damaged the precious maple dance floor. In the end the scouts decided to build their own hut in the churchyard, but the war came before it was completed.

There never is complete sweetness and light in the Church of England. There was dissent and much centred on my father. He was by nature a rebel and a foremost protagonist in the disparaged Men's Club, the centre of dissent at St Luke's. This organisation was once encouraged by the ecclesiastical hierarchy as a means of luring men from the pub. But at St Luke's it achieved the status of a subversive organisation. Its members tended to regard church attendance as an irksome rite necessary for entry to the club.

The vicar compared my father's appearance at church services with that at the Men's Club, and found it unfavourable. While my father was diligent in attending the Men's Club, averaging three or four nights a week, his presence at church was less than once a fortnight. The vicar pointed out this disparity to my father, who did not take kindly to the vicar's analysis. Disputes became bitter. Nor did the Men's Club improve domestic harmony, for Father's frequent absences were the source of recriminations from Mother. There were more quarrels over it at home than on any other topic. If the Men's Club was designed to entice men away from pubs, it also took them away from their homes.

In the New Institute, below the main hall, were rooms for billiards, table tennis and darts, the chief places of worship for members of the Men's Club. My father was a great sportsman and for year after year he had been billiards champion.

One day when Father took me along to the New Institute I saw the championship trophy. It was a large wooden shield covered with many small silver shields, each one bearing the champion's name for the year. I looked at it and proudly searched for my father's name. I searched in vain. The last engraving was dated 1932, and bore the name of the vicar. After that the miniature silver-plated shields were blank.

'Dad, why isn't your name there?' I asked Father, accusingly. He explained that it was up to the winner to pay for the engraving and he could not afford it. I felt despondent. I felt it as a slur. I still feel it as a slur. The vicar could afford to have his name inscribed on the shield and apparently gave no thought for those who could not. It was wounding to me then and is wounding to me now. I mulled over it in the years that followed. Maybe all men were equal in the sight of God but this did not extend to the C. of E. It hurt. It still hurts.

St Luke's Church Hall – the New Institute – over which there had been so much controversy, so much fund-raising effort and so much sweat, was demolished in 1998 to make way for a centre for the homeless. My brick that I bought for a shilling has yet to be returned. But I will be buying some more bricks for the new structure; they come at 25p each and seem cheap at the price.

14 The Streets of Hackney

Mr Southworth in the door of his shop in Morning Lane, in 1937. This is where we had our shoes repaired. It was an old-fashioned shop where repaired shoes were stacked in piles. *(Hackney Archives)*

T he broad acres of Hackney are a web of streets that holds within its firm grasp green parks, steepled churches, shops and terraces of grey houses. Through this maze I wound my way to friends, relations and to school.

The streets of London were also our playgrounds, but they were becoming unsafe. I was not allowed to ride my bike, a magnificent present that I had received on my eighth birthday. Secondhand, of course.

I remember offering to collect Dad's shoes from Mr Southworth the cobbler in Morning Lane. Mother looked pleased, if somewhat surprised. Then I added, 'I'll get them on my bike.' I wanted to ride it around the streets.

'Not on your bike. It's not safe. You'll get knocked down.' We wrangled for some minutes. I pointed out that I was allowed to ride the bike on

Hackney Common. 'That's different. Morning Lane is dangerous.'
The incident ended with me in a temper shouting, 'Then I won't go!'
Mother accepted my defiance calmly. 'Then don't.' It was the best way to
deal with me.

Yes, by 1936 the roads were becoming unsafe. Looking back in an old
school exercise book I see that I wrote under the heading 'Safety First':

 I must: (1) Look both ways before I cross the road.
      (2) Cross by a policeman or a beacon.
 I must not: (1) Run in the road after a ball.
      (2) Play in the road.

The all-conquering motorist was driving us children from the time-
honoured playgrounds that had been in our possession for centuries. The
traffic lights and the Belisha beacons now appearing on the roads were
menacing signs of the times. Not that we found them so as children. For us
they were mere decorations that added interest to the streets. They became the
subjects of toys and I became a proud owner of a miniature beacon. And we
continued to play those games that children had played in times past.

Brueghel would have recognised those games. There was hopscotch and
skipping for the girls and football and whipping of tops for the boys. Not
that I could whip a top along the pavements, as I lacked the necessary
coordination of mind and muscle. Both sexes ran hoops, but these were
rarely purchased from a toyshop; instead, East End children made do with
old bicycle wheels or bands from wooden barrels. The streets were our
gyms. Included in the performances were handstands, cartwheels, leapfrog
and, for the daring, walking up walls à la Donald O'Connor and finishing
with a somersault on the pavement. Even the girls joined in, tucking their
skirts into ample knickers.

Lampposts were our maypoles. Ropes were tied to the crossbar under the
lantern and from them children dangled; by running hard round they took
to the air, swept off their feet by centrifugal force. Up they went and swung
in ever-decreasing circles as the ropes twined about the lamppost. Then,
just as the children were pressed tight against the lamppost, the process
reversed, the ropes unwound and the children were flung outwards into
ever-widening circles. At the apogee, the ropes started wrapping themselves
around the lamppost again and the dangling bodies were drawn once more
inwards. And so it went on.

Then there were the gangs. Tribalism is natural in man and boy, and
ganging up has been known since the Blues and Greens formed rival
factions in the Hippodrome of New Rome. In this tradition East End men
and boys on boat race day sported a dark blue or light blue favour showing
their allegiance to either Oxford or Cambridge: an incongruous tradition, for

the varsities were so remote from the lifestyle of the East End. For whatever reason, men form adversarial groups in an arbitrary fashion. And we East End children likewise congregated into gangs and roamed the streets.

I joined the gang in Belsham Street, an L-shaped backstreet that runs from Morning Lane to Chatham Place. The leading light in the gang was Jimmy Thomas, a small wiry boy, who bathed in the reflected glory of his father, a formidable policeman of the old school. Jimmy lived in an upper-storey flat of a tenement. There was a common backyard enclosed by a brick wall breached only by a small entrance. One always entered this way and clambered up an assembly of narrow iron stairs and gangways to the back doors. On one rare occasion I was invited in, with one or two of Jimmy's friends, for tea. There, in a small sparsely furnished room, sat Jimmy's mother, immobile in a chair. It was with a shock that I realised she was paralysed. So Jimmy's policeman father acted as mother. Although he was off duty he did not shed his official zeal, and even when he was seated he emanated a massive authority. I felt uneasy, unease magnified by my father's inbred hostility to police, part of his hostility to all authority.

In the gang were Jimmy Thomas and his Belsham Street friends, with Norman Norris and Lennie Fuller from the church. I was semi-detached and Dickie Drage was not a member at all, the gang being beneath his contempt. The gang had few activities; mostly we held conferences on the iron gangways where there was talk about fighting other gangs. Rarely did it result in action and even then no one was hurt. We were paper tigers. There was a legend, related by Jimmy, of an all-girl gang who were invincible: the Amazons of Hackney. Jimmy said that they were all-in fighters who did not hesitate to bite and scratch like cats. He gave us grave advice on our tactics, if we met them. That was to run away as fast and as far as possible. From that time onward when I saw a group of girls I took evasive action. Such was my introduction to the opposite sex.

Our gang was equipped with a mobile arm, our own wooden panzer, a home-made street cart made for Lennie Fuller by his father. The chassis was a wooden soapbox fitted with four wheels, complete with axles, purloined from a discarded pram. Pram wheels were better than the old roller skates that some boys used. Steering was achieved in a simple fashion. A long board had been fastened, lengthways, under the soapbox and projected beyond it. Attached to the overhang by a single bolt was a swivelling crosspiece, carrying a pair of wheels. The driver, Lennie, sat in a cramped knees-up position in the soapbox and steered the contraption by a pair of string reins that were attached to the swivelling crosspiece. Another boy pushing from behind, generally little Norman Norris, provided motive power for this chariot.

Only once do I remember a conflict with another gang, when they invaded Belsham Street from Chatham Place. Our defences looked good.

There were two cardboard pillboxes on the pavement with a mobile force of one wooden chariot patrolling the road – the pride of the gang. Lennie and Norman manned it. We also had a formidable addition in having two cousins of Jimmy's with us. They were large, well-built blond boys, somewhat older than us, who adopted a patronising attitude toward us. We were mere kids to them.

The hostile gang appeared at the end of the street. It seemed a long way away and I was comforted. There was a long standoff as the two gangs eyed each other along the dusty grey road before battle began at long range with an exchange of stones. Roads in those days were not like those of today and abounded in dust and loose stones, so there was no shortage of missiles. At first the stone-throwing had little effect, all the stones falling short. Under those conditions I felt quite the brave warrior. Not that I did anything – I just watched, an open-mouthed spectator with a detached interest in the proceedings. The big boys said to us, 'Take cover, you boys. Leave it to us.'

As the battle warmed up, the rival gang advanced. Despite the shortening of the range, the stones the small boys threw still fell hopelessly short, but the big blond boys managed to straddle the enemy. The enemy also managed to straddle us and I felt one or two stones whistle past my person, too close for comfort. An unpleasant sensation assailed my stomach. The fighting was going against us.

The wooden fighting vehicle was hopeless. Weedy Norman could hardly push it and Lennie in a cramped sitting position was unable either to steer or throw stones from it. It zigzagged across the road, aimlessly and ineffectively. The cardboard box defences were feeble and toppled over when hit by the first stones. All our weapons, formidable in our imagination, proved useless in action.

The two blond boys, men in their own estimation, acted in a lordly and protective manner, waving us young ones to the rear (clearly we kids got in the way) while they fought a rearguard action – unsuccessfully as it proved. The cardboard pillboxes, now lying flattened on the ground, were overrun and the wooden fighting vehicle abandoned. Norman, its engine, was first to run away, leaving Lennie, hunched up in the narrow soapbox, stranded and stationary. He leapt out and our panzer was captured. The Belsham Street gang was routed. Soon it was every boy for himself. Jimmy and his big cousins scuttled through the backyard entrance and up the iron stairways towards the safety of Jimmy's home. Jimmy shouted to me. 'You can't come up. I don't want Dad to find out that I've been fighting.'

I felt hurt at my exclusion from sanctuary. But not for long, as very soon another urgent consideration came to mind: my safety. Lennie and Norman had vanished, after they left their chariot. The others, too, had evaporated somewhere in the streets of Hackney. Slowly, I realised that I was alone. I was left facing the enemy by myself. It was often my fate as a boy to be the fall guy. I considered the options. I could run up along the iron staircases outside the flats but at best I would be bottled up, and if not let in Jimmy Thomas's flat I might well be captured.

Providentially, as I crouched against a wall, I was ignored, for the hostile gang's attention was concentrated on Jimmy Thomas and co. They had retreated to an upper iron gallery outside Jimmy's front door, from where, in some safety, they hurled wordy defiance at the victorious gang below. The battle had turned into a siege where verbal abuse was exchanged. I took advantage of this distraction to slip away out of sight round the right-angled bend in Belsham Street. I decided not to linger for any counter-attack and took to my heels, leaving the shouting behind. I reached the safety of Morning Lane, panting but relieved.

I never returned to that gang after it had lost the Battle of Belsham Street, but instead took up with some boys from nearby Devonshire Street, a road that ran parallel to Darnley Road. We were just three boys with no leader who roamed the streets at random. My companions were rough diamonds. Often we would cluster outside the Devonshire Club, where Jack Solomons promoted boxing, and look at posters of young boxing hopefuls in fighting postures. My friends knew all about them.

Once, for nothing better to do, I led these boys in a 'crusade' against the Jews of Darnley Road, my neighbours. We laid siege to them in their own front gardens. Taunts were exchanged and then missiles, toy arrows from primitive bows and paper wads from elastic bands. The mutual exchange of missiles was quite ineffective. Now, I like to think that this episode was no more than simple boyish fun, but was it more? Was it because Jews were different? Or was it a mild form of anti-Semitism? Whatever it was, this unprovoked aggression on my part made my conscience uneasy. My mood changed. I was determined to make peace with my neighbours. But how?

One sunny day, when looking up from our front airy, I spied two Jewish boys, Ashley Kossoff and Buddy Matthews, playing in the middle of Darnley Road. A feeling of goodwill welled up in my breast. I resolved to make friends with them. I racked my brains for an idea. I looked in my toy cupboard and found a pair of Father's Indian clubs. With one in each hand I ascended the airy steps with trepidation. I blurted out, 'How about a game of rounders?' They accepted and soon our past hostilities were forgotten as we played an enjoyable game. Peace was made and we became friends. But there was a price to pay: Father's Indian clubs, which he prized, suffered abrasion. He was not pleased when he saw them and I thought that he had made a fuss about nothing.

Despite this outbreak of peace, certain issues were not resolved. I had primitive theological arguments with Ashley outside his house next door. He refused to believe in Jesus Christ, while I denied the historic existence of Adam and Eve. We argued hotly but finally we compromised and I agreed to believe in Adam and Eve if Ashley would believe in Jesus. I commend this approach to religious leaders.

We boys of Darnley Road would meet in each other's houses: in my basement flat, to play trains; in the bare and empty basement of Ashley's house next door, where the only lighting was by a bat's wing gas burner. Buddy Matthews lived in a basement flat on the other side of Darnley Road and there we gathered to play cards or stones and to gossip about sport and the news. Ashley was bright-eyed, quick and intelligent but Buddy was the opposite, the slowest boy that I have ever known. He drawled in a belaboured speech and was generally thought to be stupid. At school in a class of forty-four, he would be forty-fourth. But, as I remember, he was inventive and most of the store of games we played came from him. And as it turned out he was not stupid but just very lazy, as would be proved one day.

Sometimes we went to Hackney Downs to play cricket, where I provided bat, stumps and balls. Although I was the poorest of the group I seemed to have all the toys. On one occasion we invaded the General Post Office in Paragon Lane. Ashley pedalled my model racing car through the foyer, followed by little Michael, the boy next door with two-tone hair – he had a streak of blond hair amid a shock of otherwise dark hair – who rode my tricycle. I was too big for either and anyway decided to stay in safety

Shops in Kingsland High Street, 1933. *(Hackney Archives)*

outside. As it turned out I had not thought things through and my caution was in vain. After a few goes the authorities objected and we were chased along Paragon Road, little Michael pedalling fast and furiously, but to no avail. He leapt from the tricycle, leaving it on its side on the pavement. Likewise, Ashley abandoned my toy motor car and fled on foot. Although I was well ahead of the field, I had no option but to return to my deserted toys. Thus I fell into the hands of authority. I protested my innocence, which was true enough, but authority bellowed, 'Whose are these?', and I replied in a small thin voice, 'Mine.' As usual I was the fall guy and, not for the first or last time, a policeman of the *Dixon of Dock Green* variety took me home to Mother. But he did help me with the toys. I was crestfallen but when Father heard about it he did not chide me but laughed out loud.

Today I am not sure of my motives in forming friendships with the Jewish boys. Was I repelled by open expressions of anti-Semitism around me or was it that I sought middle-class friends? I suspect that I was moving slowly from a working-class ethic to that of the middle class. And was that why I abandoned the Belsham Street gang and the Devonshire Street boys?

There was uneasiness in the streets of East London in the autumn of 1936. Sinister men in black shuffled along Mare Street with pamphlets and placards. In the dusk they hung about at the entrances to Woolworths and Marks & Spencers. I felt vaguely threatened. These were the Blackshirts, the Fascists of Britain: tribalism was not confined to small boys. Their centre was Ridley Road and Kingsland High Street.

My Jewish friends told me that these Fascists, protected by police, had marched through Jewish streets; that they had overturned the stalls of Jewish street traders, and thrown bricks through plate-glass windows of Jewish-owned shops. I was told that sometimes at night there would be a knock on a door with the shouting of threats. Living nearby, unknown to me at the time, was another Jewish boy, Harold Pinter, and some of his plays reflect the fears of those days. Nevertheless, to me these disquieting happenings were but unpleasant rumours and something that I did not feel or experience.

Then one day the nebulous became flesh. It was at morning service in St Luke's when a group of Fascists dressed in smart black uniforms paraded into the church in tight formation. They strutted with synchronised steps to an empty pew and sat down. The vicar was struck as nearly dumb as one of the cloth can be. Although the Fascists were well behaved they were as insensitive as clockwork soldiers and I felt their menace. They seemed like an army of occupation in the church. I was fearful, but others in the congregation were resentful and angry. Their church, their sanctuary had been invaded by aliens. 'It oughtn't to be allowed' was a common reaction, but the vicar explained that they were within their rights.

That autumn tensions exploded into mass violence. One night my father came home with the news of the battle of Cable Street – that now legendary battle which stopped the Blackshirts in their tracks. Once again the Fascists had marched through the streets of the East End. Once again the police protected them. But the anti-Fascists were prepared and massed behind barricades. The might of the Fascists and the Metropolitan Police was thwarted that day. My father remarked that the Jews had done us all a good turn but, of course, not all the anti-Fascists were Jews. Soon afterwards the government banned uniforms. This took the steam out of the movement and never again would Fascists lord it or march like an army into a church.

The Crystal Palace in ruins. *(LMA)*

One evening late in the year, Father called us out into the street to witness a strange red glow on the southern horizon of the night sky. Next day we knew that the Crystal Palace had been burnt down. All that was left was one tower that stood proud above the wreckage. The Crystal Palace had been built in Hyde Park, when the Empire was at its peak, for the 1851 Great Exhibition, a marvel of prefabrication. It was a symbol of Britain's industrial greatness, for in that era our manufacturing and financial wealth far outstripped that of all other countries. Then Britain was the superpower and the motto of those times was 'Pax Britannica'. The destruction of Crystal Palace was another dark omen for an ever-beleaguered Empire. And some remembered the imperial crown lying in the gutter.

15 Submission of a King

I was standing with a huddle of children beneath an all-mains wireless that sat high upon a shelf in a small bare hall of the New Institute. In front of us, seated on hard wooden chairs, were the adults. I had come along with Mum and Dad to listen to the broadcast of the man who had once been king. Like many in the Hackney of those days we lacked an all-mains wireless set. Chairs were scraped as we waited for the broadcast, tense and with the anticipation of dismay.

The abdication crisis came suddenly, just after the Crystal Palace had burnt down. There was an American lady called Mrs Simpson who the king wanted to marry but couldn't because she was married already. At least that's what Mr Baldwin had said and he was Prime Minister.

In the New Institute we chatted as we waited for the broadcast. Then someone stepped forward and switched the wireless on. Silence fell as the wireless warmed up. After two minutes or so it hissed its readiness. Knobs were twiddled, producing at first only whistles and wailing shrieks. These died away as the national station came through clear. A grave Scottish voice announced a Prince Edward. Prince Edward: who was he? There were murmurs. 'The King, of course,' said someone. 'The ex-king, you mean.' Then there was quiet again. It was one of those memorable broadcasts, although I do not know quite why. The King, or Prince as he was by then, talked in clipped, strained tones in a romantic vein. Apparently he could not continue without the woman he loved. So that was it.

The abdication was a curiously disturbing event for me, which tarnished the magic of king and empire. The order of things had been stood on its head. Once I had rejoiced in the enchantment of majesty. Nothing dampened my enthusiasm. I had revelled in the patriotic song 'Land of Hope and Glory', often trilling it aloud and getting very cross when my mother teased me by countering with the parody, 'Land of Soapy Water'. Her mocking made me furious. I think my excess of zeal disturbed her. I was always an earnest little chap.

Of kings and princes I had had enough. We had three kings in that year of 1936 and that was plenty. Christmas was approaching and with other children in the school playground I chanted happily the refrain:

> Hark the Herald Angels sing
> Mrs Simpson's pinched our King.

16   The Crowning of a King

In 1936 there had been no armour against the icy hand of fate, and sceptres and crowns had tumbled down. It had begun with a king dying and ended with a king abdicating – the year of the three kings. But there had been a royal queen, that great liner the *Queen Mary*, who was to endure. She had made her maiden voyage in May and at school all talk was about her and the *Normandie*, her French rival, which held the coveted Blue Riband for the fastest crossing of the Atlantic. The question, hotly argued with my friends, was could the *Queen Mary* wrest this prize away from the French ship?

One day Derek Smith came round to Darnley Road with a tattered magazine and we pored over pictures of the *Queen Mary*. 'Why it's like a palace!' I exclaimed as we gazed, goggling together, at sumptuous art deco interiors – opulent pillared lounges, sophisticated lighting, sweeping staircases and chased bronze doors. All in a ship! Lounging at the tables were passengers dressed like Ginger Rogers and Fred Astaire. No doubt they were whiling away the four or five days it took to cross the Atlantic. Oh! those leisurely days of travel in the irretrievable past.

This floating grand hotel, with its affluent clientele, was far removed from our underprivileged lives endured in grey streets and small rooms. Not that such thoughts occurred to Derek Smith or me, for we were simply captivated by the magic of the *Queen Mary*. Derek Smith avidly discussed the ship's statistics. He was like that, being an intellectual boy. He told me that she displaced 81,000 tons and was capable of 28 knots. So exciting then, but what is 28 knots in this day of 500–600 knot jets? 'She must be the biggest ship in the world.' But Derek Smith, a wiseacre among boys, maintained otherwise. The *Normandie*, he asserted, was larger at 83,000 tons. 'Then she's faster.' Again Derek Smith disabused me. The *Normandie* was half a knot faster. He was a precise boy. But despite his scepticism the *Queen Mary* did succeed in gaining the Blue Riband for a time and my pride in Great Britain was restored. However, there was to be a ding-dong battle with the *Normandie* for that prize.

I began to take interest in the air. Some years before I had seen the silvery shape of the *Graf Zeppelin* float gracefully across the sky of Frampton Park Road. Its vast size startled me; it was as large as a liner, and airborne. But it had not returned and to me it was no more than an object. There were also little biplanes that occasionally droned in London's skies, Dragon Rapides as I recall. Sometimes I would see one framed in a classroom window when, bored with a lesson, I found the blank sky more interesting than the teacher.

The Birdman is forgotten now, but all attention was upon him when he came to England in 1936. His name was Clem Sohn, and he dominated the news. He was one of the last of that long line of brave fools who followed in the flight path of Icarus. The Birdman was a parachutist, but with the added gimmick of a pair of cloth wings that stretched between his hands and his feet. It gave him a bat-like appearance. With this equipment he claimed to fly, and since no one was in the sky with him at the time, it was difficult to refute his claims.

The shops were full of model birdmen. Derek Smith, my intellectual friend, was the first to buy one and I soon followed suit. They were really an elaborate form of paper dart that could be propelled into the air with a band of elastic. Looking back now it is difficult to see why we were all so excited over the Birdman; his act was as archaic as the medieval tower leapers. The real wonder of aviation was unknown to us, for Whittle was secretly working on his jet engine that would change the world. Yet all we could do was goggle at the antiquated Birdman. In truth I expect we all recognised him for what he was – a showman, and a showman like the high-wire artist who dances with death. It was death that accompanied him on his flights and drew us towards him. And death was soon to take him. In France the next year the Birdman made his last jump. His parachutes failed to open and that was that. Derek Smith told me so when he came round to discuss a project for producing a magazine using a jelly graph. Together we were full of imaginative ideas that never materialised.

All that was in 1936. Now it was 1937, a different year, a terminal period of calm as it proved, between turbulent years of the past and what was to come.

As 1937 moved on Coronation fever grew. The shops filled with Coronation kitsch: flags, souvenirs, guidebooks and commemorative pottery. I became a victim of that obsession to preserve the transient in the amber of memorabilia. My collecting instinct revived and I bought a toy royal coach, ornate and gilded, and a Coronation throne, complete with a slide-in Scone stone. The school gave me an LCC (London County Council) commemorative mug. These objects were added to my museum, the upturned fish tank. My Coronation treasures joined my jubilee collection and the William IV shilling. Alas, they all disappeared in the blitz, together with my toy train set.

As the day approached excitement grew in both adults and children. The East End of London always made a great show of these things. No class of people could be further removed from the pomp and circumstance of

A souvenir mug of the 1937 Coronation given to schoolchildren by the LCC. (Author's collection)

monarchy. There was no pomp about the people of the East End. The pride of place implicit in the monarchy and all its trappings was far removed from our egalitarian and earthy world. Yet no class of people was more patriotic or more prone to wave the Union Jack. Perhaps the drabness of East End life made us all seek a little colour.

The Coronation was the occasion for a grand gala of street parties. Each terraced house vied with its neighbour in the garishness of decoration, for in the poorer areas flags, pennants and bunting were displayed from windows and flung across the streets from window to window. The grey streets disappeared under a flush of red, white and blue. I had long looked forward to the Coronation street party. The street tea parties were great fun for East End children but they were exclusive to the poorer streets. Darnley Road was too posh to have one so, not wishing to miss out, I put my name down for the one in Stevens Avenue. Trestle tables were placed end-to-end for the whole length of the street and covered with brightly coloured paper. These were to be loaded with sweet things, buns, fairy cakes, jellies and other sugary delights. But it did not happen.

Alas, we had reckoned without the unpatriotic weather. Came the great day and came the drizzle and showers, so in the event the 'street party' was held in the church hall. This was not the same as having it in the gaily

The Coronation of 1937, as portrayed on the cover of the *Radio Times*. (*The C.R.W. Nevinson Estate/Bridgeman Art Gallery and the Radio Times Magazine*)

bedecked streets. The hall was dull and overcrowded, full of milling children, with adults trying to bring order out of chaos. Decorations were sparse. Wooden trestle tables were covered in white paper and plates of sandwiches and cakes and mugs of tea deposited on them. At the end of the party each of us was given a Coronation mug, which was some consolation for the weather. Otherwise it all turned out rather ordinary. It was not the exciting affair I had expected. Once more I had been deprived of my street party and there were to be no others.

Father, not surprisingly, had volunteered for Coronation duty. He was a Rover Scout and they were used as auxiliaries to control crowds, provide first aid and generally help. Father regaled us with details; for him, being on duty was great fun. He went on and on about 'iron rations'. These were concentrated foods, including chocolate. Father emphasised that there were no fluids to be taken, for obvious reasons.

One of his jobs was to keep the crush barriers clear, and he later delighted in telling, and retelling, the story of one obstreperous individual. He was a little chap who clasped the barrier and could not be persuaded by my father to let go. Father said, 'So I called a copper, a huge chap well over 6 foot. Taller than me. He said to the little chap, "Get off that barrier!" And the little chap shook his head. So do you know what the copper did?' My father grinned from ear to ear; he was clearly hugely amused at the memory. 'Why, he picked him up by the scruff of his neck with one hand like this,' my father demonstrated, 'and laid him out with an almighty uppercut like this.' My father's hand swept upwards. 'Then the copper called out to the St John's Ambulance man, "Casualty!"' My father enjoyed this incident, which seemed straight out of a cartoon by H.E. Bateman, for he relished this form of direct action. 'Of course I couldn't do it myself. I would have been arrested.' He grinned broadly and I knew he wished he could have done it himself.

The premises of James Brooke & Son, Home Furnishers, Hackney, decorated to celebrate the Coronation. The shop was full of art deco furniture. *(Hackney Archives)*

The rest of his reminiscences were run-of-the-mill duties, although he did remark on the great length of the lavatory queues. As for the Coronation procession, my father hardly seemed to have noticed it. For most of us the Coronation was something we experienced second-hand. We read about it in the newspapers the day after and eventually saw it on the newsreels some weeks later. We had our parties and collected memorabilia and that was enough. The rest was left to our imagination. We did not have to see the event to experience it.

This was the age of cigarette cards and I assembled an album on the Coronation courtesy of John Player & Sons. From it I learnt of the trappings of royalty, of the Earl Marshal of England, Garter King of Arms, Lord Lyon King of Arms and other worthies dressed in strange but impressive attire. Their jobs were peculiar and concerned with such things as honour and precedence. This did not mean much to me. Others seemed to have non-jobs such as the City Marshal, once responsible for keeping order in the streets of London who, so I read, now had nothing to do – the police had taken over – but performed 'ceremonial' duties, whatever they were. I was baffled. These jobs were so unlike the workaday jobs of my family.

I learnt of the Orders of Knighthood with their odd names, Garter, Thistle and Bath. Garters, thistles and baths! What strange subjects for knighthoods! The cigarette cards showed men attired in elaborate garb that exuded an archaic grandeur, a contrast to the drab thirties world about me.

The Coronation stirred my interest in contemporary events and I started a scrapbook. It was filled mainly with newspaper cuttings of the *Spithead Review*, the last unashamed worship of Empire and might. The cuttings are faded now and it takes imagination to see in them gaily bedecked warships with flags strung from mast to mast and mast to prow. But these grey, blurred cuttings are coloured sharply in my memory, as are the lights that festooned the masts and conning towers at night and which I never saw. There were a few ships of other navies. In my scrapbook I pasted a photograph of the *Graf Spee*, the German pocket battleship, below which a caption stated that it 'looks and is a very powerful cruiser'. It had about it a sinister beauty but on the whole the handful of foreign ships merely served to emphasise the might of our navy. Who could doubt the reality of our seaborne Empire!

Newsreels of that time emphasised our maritime power. They showed grey-grim battleships steaming in false glory, one after the other in line of battle, an endless progression of apparent might. They showed them in action hurling black broadside after black broadside at some unknown enemy cowering beneath the shelter of the distant horizon. All a delusion. Power lay in the air, yet I do not remember an aircraft carrier; if there were any, I doubt if their flat tops excited much interest.

Battleships obsessed me and later I came across a book on the fleets of the world, which I eagerly devoured. I knew that the British fleet was the greatest in the world, or so I was told. I thumbed the pages rapidly to confirm these facts. I looked at the British battleships. There were twelve of them, more than in the German and Japanese navies. Then I turned to the USA fleet. It came as a shock when I counted out fifteen American battleships. Three more than in our fleet. This could not be so. Desperately I turned the pages backwards and forwards and checked again and again, but the numbers would not change. Then there came dawning hope.

I counted three British battlecruisers, essentially fast battleships. That made fifteen capital ships in each navy. I was relieved. Moreover, among the three battlecruisers was the 'mighty *Hood*', the greatest ship in the world, so we were told. I looked up its armament; it carried eight 15-inch guns. Match that, I thought, and turned to the American ships. A second shock came as I saw that many carried the larger 16-inch guns, often nine of them. Then I looked back to the British ships and most carried only eight 15-inch guns. There were only two to match the US fleet, the *Nelson* and *Rodney*, with nine 16-inch guns each. At that moment I realised that my country was no longer the greatest sea power in the world. The lonely agony of Jack Cornwell dying on that slippery grey deck at Jutland, the heroic symbol of Britain's naval supremacy, was forgotten. My mind slipped back to that chart on the wall, and those parallel bands that showed the British Empire was just one leading power among many. Perhaps she was not even that. But the film makers came to my rescue with *Victoria the Great*, which depicted the glory of the Victorian Empire with Anna Neagle striding with full majesty through the stately film. More ominous was *Fire over England*, an England threatened by the might of the Spanish Armada.

17 My Fortune is Told

At first I did not know ambition. I had been happy enough playing with my toys and my friends. My ambition was fathered by fear. It came when I woke from the dream of childhood and saw the world about me, and my position in it. I did not like what I saw. I saw an uncertain future for myself in the fate of the working-class boys who ended up going to the senior school, where they became a bunch of ragged, shouting semi-hooligans.

My ambition focused on one objective: the gaining of a scholarship to grammar school. But so far I had achieved little and Miss Gough's gloomy assessment of my abilities on the day I left Morning Road School seemed depressingly correct when I first went to Orchard. My performance grew worse and I struggled in my class of poor and not very bright boys from the East End of London. But I was persistent and did not give up hope. I moved on into the class of Mr Freeman. Mr Freeman was a man of understanding and sympathy. He was the first teacher to realise that I was not an absolute dunce. This revelation came after some poor test results, when I had burst into tears of disappointment and frustration. My mother went to see him. He told her not to worry and that it was good that I was upset. It showed that I was persistent. 'That', he said, 'is Alan's strength. Of course, Alan goes his own way. He does not solve problems using the methods he is taught but works out his own peculiar solutions. I find it difficult to understand them but he often gets the right results. Don't give up hope, Mrs Wilson. He's nearly as good as Susman and Phillips.' These were acknowledged as the most intelligent boys in the class, of this there was no doubt. Mr Freeman's remark came as a surprise to Mother. He told her that Susman and Phillips were sure to get scholarships. 'With Alan, on the other hand, well, he is erratic and it will depend on what mood he is in on the day.' This conversation was relayed back to me by Mother and gave me hope and confidence. I tried harder.

The yearly school examination results came in April. I was in for a surprise. I had shot up the class from somewhere in the middle of a class of forty to fifth behind Phillips, Susman, Hall and Rosner. Written on my report was the simple statement: 'Alan has plenty of ability and should win a scholarship.' This amazed my mother, as well as pleasing her. I was surprised but happy. I could hardly believe it. For the first time I was given hope.

My 1937 Orchard School report.
(Author's collection)

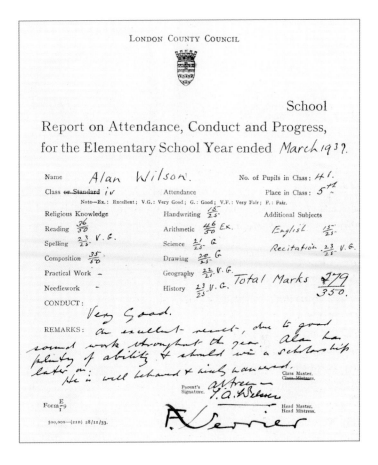

LONDON COUNTY COUNCIL

School

Report on Attendance, Conduct and Progress,

for the Elementary School Year ended *March 1937.*

Name *Alan Wilson.*   No. of Pupils in Class: *41.*

Class or Standard *iv*   Attendance   Place in Class: *5th.*

Note—Ex.: Excellent; V.G.: Very Good; G.: Good; V.F.: Very Fair; F.: Fair.

Religious Knowledge   Handwriting *15/25*   Additional Subjects

Reading *36/50*   Arithmetic *46/50 Ex.*   *English 15/25.*

Spelling *23/25 V.G.*   Science *21/25 G*

Composition *35/50*   Drawing *20/25 G*   *Recitation 23/25 V.G.*

Practical Work —   Geography *22/25 V.G.*   *Total Marks 279/350.*

Needlework —   History *23/25 V.G.*

CONDUCT: *Very Good.*

REMARKS: *An excellent result, due to good sound work throughout the year. Alan has plenty of ability & should win a scholarship later on: He is well behaved & nicely mannered.*

Parent's Signature. *A. Wilson*   Class Master. Class Mistress.

Form E/9   Head Master. Head Mistress.

500,000—(21D) 28/11/33.

Some time after this Mr Verrier, the headmaster, started taking an interest in me and considered that I had now become a scholarship prospect. Mr Verrier gave us boys a pamphlet of the LCC entitled 'Now You Are Ten'. I took it home and looked at it with my mother. The booklet charted the way to the land of dreams. On one page was a diagram mapping the paths of advancement, which were for me also escape routes. We saw that three roads emanated from the box of the junior school: the left led to a grammar school, the middle to a central school and the right to a senior school.

The authorities liked to pretend that these alternatives were all equal and pontificated in their foolish wisdom. They preached in soothing terms that those awful senior schools were just as good as grammar schools but were for those who were gifted with their hands rather than their heads. So much nonsense. I knew that they just taught you wood-work, metal craft and other handicraft. A little above senior schools were central schools, which offered secretarial courses. As far as I was concerned this was a fall-back position, for the plum, I knew, was the grammar school.

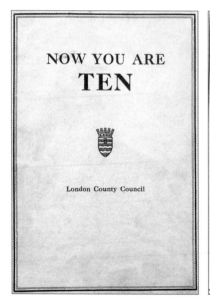

'Now You Are Ten.
The way to the future for a
working class boy!'
An LCC pamphlet that
I received when I was ten
years old.

I was only dimly aware of what happened in a grammar school, but it was said they taught maths and Latin there. That much my father had picked up from reading about the boys of Greyfriars in the *Magnet*. My father, like many working-class boys and men, was absorbed by the happenings of Harry Wharton and co., not forgetting Billy Bunter, in that fossilised world of Greyfriars which, if it corresponded to anything, was a Victorian ethic. Yet this was the 1930s!

Mother and I studied the figure in 'Now You Are Ten' again and again and I became aware of roads that lay beyond these secondary schools to higher levels, to junior technical colleges, technical colleges and, at the summit, universities. But what were these august establishments?

I asked, 'Mum, what's a university?' Mum was momentarily lost for words as she gave it some thought. Unusual. 'It's where clever people go after they leave school.' I picked that up at once. It seemed far better to me than doing those awful jobs boys did such as being errand boys or serving in shops. I thought it over. 'How do you get in?' I asked. 'It says here you have to matriculate.' My ambition was now clearly defined: first win a scholarship to a grammar school and then matriculate to a university. The scholarship would open all doors. Fail that and the door to advancement would be barred against me forever – at the age of ten.

I mulled it over. I dreamed my dreams. Of winning a scholarship, of going to university and gaining a degree. Not that I knew what a university was or what it was for. I only knew that it was the top of the tree.

My ambition was not for myself alone. Even more it was for my parents. My father's own ambitions had long been quenched, leaving him only with disillusionment. My mother had a simple faith in me. Ambition for their only son had become the salt of their lives. But ambition is a misguided philosophy. Life begins as a great adventure but deepens as we tread along that road. All we can do is to travel hopefully.

The time had come round for the church bazaar. The hall was packed with a throng of people. I threaded slowly through a clutter of stalls, hunting for bargains. Rows of stalls were stacked high with all the bric-a-brac and I played a game of guessing the use of the more arcane items. I stared vacantly at women endlessly turning over piles of jumble like a farmer tedding hay. I was as bored as could be until I spied the gaily coloured booth of a fortune-teller. The booth was decorated with the silvery iconography of astrology: stars, crescent moons and pentagons. My imagination was stirred. I stood before the booth in indecision; should I go in or not? Should I have my fortune told? I had a pressing desire to know. I needed moral support for my burgeoning ambition, and to build up confidence in my ability to succeed. But to have my fortune told was a challenge to my disbelief. These thoughts chased each other around in my mind. I hesitated, still shuffling aimlessly before the fortune-teller's booth. In the end I decided to have my fortune told. I had to know my fate. I had to put my question.

I entered the fortune-teller's booth with some trepidation, and recognised the fortune-teller as none other than Mr Shillum, a close friend of my father, a company secretary: very respectable, a gaunt man with a grave face, about as far away from a gypsy as it was possible to imagine. Mr Shillum, a fortune-teller! I was taken aback. He looked incongruous in a fortune-teller's shawl! A fortune-teller should be a fortune-teller, not Mr Shillum, I thought. It was all very confusing and I tried to suspend disbelief. I was determined to go ahead and ask my question. I tried to go along with the illusion. There was only one question I wanted to ask him. I wanted to be certain of my ability. I wanted to know: how would I get on? It was not a question I would have asked a year earlier. I kept on asking him, how will I get on in life? He was bland. He tried to change the subject. He went on about other things. I kept bringing him back to the point time and time again. I knew he was being evasive, and I knew why. He did not have the answer I wished to hear. He hemmed and hawed. He spoke soothingly. He told me I would do quite well, but that I must not expect too much. He told me not to worry and that I would have a good life. I asked him about the scholarship. Would I win one? He told me that winning a scholarship was very difficult. Most probably I would go to a central school. I left the booth depressed, with my earlier illusions of success quite gone. So that, I thought, was Mr Shillum's opinion of me. Was I a mediocrity? I did not feel good about it. I wandered about feeling depressed, although my determination remained. The fire of ambition burnt within me as strongly as ever.

18   Home

In autumn that year Mr Hubble raised the rent again. My parents looked into the matter of buying one of the new houses. This was the thirties, the age of the ideal home, when ordinary people first thought of buying their own houses. So it was that my parents would peruse the newspapers and see the attractive new houses, which to them represented a kind of paradise. Not much to ask. But try as they might, my parents were not able to get the sums to add up. My father's wage of £3 10s was just not enough. My mother was given the opportunity of a job as a supervisor in a small clothes company. But Granny would have to look after me at lunch-times. This she refused to do. She was an old-fashioned lady who believed in traditional values: that women should not go out to work. So we lived on in the basement of 12 Darnley Road. And, somehow, the extra rent was managed.

At the end of 1937 we rented our first all-mains wireless set, a Philco as I remember, which came with magic eye tuning! There were no heavy accumulators to carry round to the electrical shop each week for recharging and no expensive HT batteries to buy. The set was just plugged into the light socket and a few minutes after switching on, 'warming up' we called it, the stations came through.

I cannot say that I found much on radio interesting, at least not during the day. There was Reginald Foort playing away at the cinema organ interminably. Later, Sandy Macpherson was to take over from him, in much the same vein. Not much of an advance on the Black and White Minstrels, *Colonel Bogey* and *In a Monastery Garden* that once squeaked from my gramophone.

Of the children's programmes I remember only *Toy Town* with dear old Larry the Lamb. I would still listen to *Toy Town* today, but alas it is not in the modern mould for children. Radio Luxembourg had come on the air and caused a stir. The advertisements were a novelty and one listened to them as much as anything else. But after a time the novelty palled, for the station offered a constant diet of light music.

On Saturday we listened to *In Town Tonight*. One Michael Standing would step into the mighty roar of London's traffic and quell it. I seem to remember some ragged-trousered street philosopher pushing his barrow and scattering words of doubtful wisdom. On Monday there was *Monday Night at Seven* with its little jingle:

It's Monday Night at Seven
Oh can't you hear the chimes?
They're telling you to take an easy chair
To settle by the fireside,
Look at your Radio Times
For Monday Night at Seven's on the air

This jingle conjures up the cosy atmosphere of those times, and such times can never recur. They belong to the irrecoverable and elusive past. The fireside has gone and with it the soft fireside light. Central heating has seen to that. And if we draw our chairs up to face anything it will be disturbing television. A kind of innocence has vanished from this world. Then we had technology in moderation. We never thought it could go much further. No atomic bombs and no computer games. Cosiness was the theme. Perhaps it was an unconscious, defensive womb, a protection against the unspoken fear of a coming war and disruptive change. Cosy days they were, but in that year the first refugees from the Spanish Civil War were beginning to arrive in England.

A typical suburban house of the 1930s such as my parents dreamed of.
(*Author's collection*)

19   An Uneasy Spring

The last year of peace, 1938, opened to the quaint and archaic strains of the 'Lambeth Walk', a melody that came from the show *Me and My Girl*. It was a memorable ditty with a dance.

> Any time you're Lambeth way,
> Any evening, any day,
> You'll find us all doin' the Lambeth Walk, Oi!
> Ev'ry little Lambeth girl,
> With her little Lambeth pal,
> You'll find 'em all doin' the Lambeth Walk, Oi!
> Ev'rything free and easy,
> Do as you darn well pleasy,
> Why don't you make your way there,
> Go there, stay there,
> Once you get down Lambeth way,
> Ev'ry evening, ev'ry day,
> You'll find yourself doin' the Lambeth Walk, Oi!

We schoolboys took to the ditty and pranced up and down, rolling with the tune. When we came to the 'Oi!' we shouted and jerked our right arms back with a thumbs-up gesture. We did it in the playground and in the streets but mainly I remember it being performed on the broad pavement outside the Paragon Shoe Works in Retreat Place. The 'Lambeth Walk' was strangely out of place with its old-fashioned cockney certainty in that uncertain swing era of 1938. It harked back to an earlier age, the Edwardian era of the music hall when the triumphs of the Empire were fresh in the mind. The tune was a swansong of that departed world and a strange overture for what was to follow. It was against these strains that Hitler marched into Austria.

The Austrian Anschluss marked another stage in my journey from the dream of childhood. I began to read newspapers and their sad tidings more deeply.

The cartoons made the greatest impression. One showed Hitler and Mussolini sitting astride caterpillar tanks that rode the world stage. They were accompanied by strutting armoured soldiers, grotesque Roman warriors encased in breastplates and antique plumed helmets; brutal looking, carrying bouquets of crossed artillery pieces and heaped-up machine guns, the sinister armorials of war. These goings-on were witnessed by a bemused Mr Chamberlain, stiff in his winged collar and clutching a feeble umbrella.

The cartoon that made the greatest impression on me was one of quiet and strange content. A lady was sitting in a chair, dressed in an archaic style; but despite her regal bearing she was shackled to her seat. The caption underneath read, 'The Rape of Austria'. At the time the scene meant little to me; I did not know what Austria was or the meaning of the word 'rape'. Yet I remember that cartoon to this day. I knew that something terrible had happened and that the world was a sinister place.

But I had more personal things to worry about that spring. I was due to sit what were known as the preliminary examinations, taken before the scholarship proper, to weed out the weaker brethren. A week or two before the preliminaries I went down with tonsillitis, yet again. It was becoming a chronic illness of mine. There was some talk of removing my tonsils. They were not good. I was to suffer all the torments of medicine in those inter-war years, for Victorian remedies had not yet passed away. And I had two Victorian grandmothers.

Nan's 'cure' was to toast a slice of bread till it charred and then soak it in malt vinegar. This soggy and revolting mess was then fastened around my neck by a cloth. An odious smell of hot vinegar and burnt bread assailed my nostrils and made me feel nauseous. As time passed it became cold and dank and the smell, now of sweat combined with vinegar, became even more revolting. The charred bread, as it dried, hardened into an abrasive board that chafed my neck which, already softened by hot vinegar, became spongy, red and raw. So much for Nan's contribution to the science of medicine.

Gran's remedy was an equally nauseous home-made concoction, but of a different nature to Nan's 'cure', which it complemented. A large onion was cut and brown demerara sugar layered between the slices. This onion-sugar sandwich was placed in a large saucer. As it matured, a thick evil-smelling brown liquid oozed out and dribbled down the outside of the onion as globules collected in a pool at the bottom of the saucer. This disgusting brown liquid was fed to me by the spoonful at regular intervals. It tasted much as it looked and I came to dread medicine time.

These repellent remedies were powerful incentives for an invalid to get well and therein lies the secret of Victorian medicine – unpleasantness. In the event, these unsavoury nostrums had little effect on my tonsillitis.

I grew more desperate as the day of the examination came near. Every half-hour my mother, impatient as always, would hurriedly feel my brow, as if the condition would vanish that quickly. My whole future depended on winning a scholarship and I was not to be balked by a mere fever. I was determined to go to the examination, fever or not. So one day I got up, declared that I was better, and staggered about the room for an hour or two before retreating exhausted to bed. A desperate gloom settled on the household. Mother, in a doom-laden voice, said that I wasn't meant to get a scholarship, the fatalistic attitude of the working class. Fortunately, she shrugged off her fatalism and consulted Mr Verrier, the headmaster. He solved the problem in a trice. 'No need to worry, Mrs Wilson,' he said. 'Since he is ill, I am allowed to give him a pass in the preliminaries and he can sit the scholarship examination in the summer.' Solving intractable problems seemed so easy when you knew how.

Later that summer I took the scholarship examination on which all depended. My mother said, 'Don't be disappointed if you fail.' I promised her, 'No I won't, but I'll cry my blooming eyes out.'

The examination was held in the assembly hall, which had been filled with rows of desks for the occasion. I sat at one of them. All was deadly quiet. Mr Verrier and his assistants stood by a table at one end of the hall, all quite still. I looked around. For once there were girls as well as boys present. I saw Rosemary, she who was born on the same day as I, she whom I had loved at a distance and to whom I had never uttered one word. I gazed admiringly at her chubby cheeks. Then there was movement as the examination papers were distributed.

To my surprise, I enjoyed the examination. The excitement was pleasant and the flow of adrenalin served to inspire rather than confuse. I sailed through the general paper, more of a game than an examination. The English paper was easier than I had expected, for it put emphasis on clear thinking rather than on the niceties of composition. I described the superiority of the horse-drawn cart over the petrol van for delivering milk, emphasising that the horse was more adept at stopping and starting than the petrol engine. So far so good. But then came the arithmetic and I faltered. I failed to perceive that a square with sides of two units is four times rather than twice as big as one with sides of one unit. I realised my mistake as soon as the papers were collected. As I trudged home I turned the mistake over and over again in my mind. Would I now fail the scholarship as a result of this slip? Would my future be compromised by just one silly error?

I began to take an interest in cricket in 1938, when the Australians came on tour. I asked my father who were the great cricketers. He said W.G. Grace and Hobbs, but Grace, it seemed, was dead and Hobbs had retired. So I asked who was the best today. Well, there was Hammond and Bradman, who was one of those awful Australians who didn't like body-line bowling. Father then got quite excited about the subject of 'body-line'

and Aussies who were calling it intimidatory. My father put their protests
down to them being bad losers.

I took no notice of the Australians' cricketing tour until the Oval Test in
late August. My friends at school became very excited. An English batsman
had been at the crease for three days and, against the best bowler in the
world, had hit over 364 runs, a world record. Was it Hammond, I asked?
He seemed to be the only available hero who was not dead, retired or an
Australian. No, it was Hutton, not a name in my canon, and I was
disappointed. Schoolboys like the old heroes and new ones take time to be
accepted.

The match is history now and for a time the world, within the green
confines of the cricket field, was safe. The England team's score of 907 runs
declared was momentous. England won the match by an innings and
hundreds of runs. It was just as well that we had won something then, for
we were not going to win anything else for some time. Looking back, I see
that the match had an air of unreality about it that has not diminished
with time. Soon the white figures plying bat against ball disappeared and
the safe, green fields of the Oval faded away. Dark figures with spades were
scarring out trenches in the green swards of Victoria Park. The balmy
cricket days of August had gone with the autumn leaves and the gathering
crisis over Czechoslovakia erupted in September. My father forgot about
body-line.

20   Talk of War

War. The talk was of war: of the war that had gone and the war that might yet come. It stirred Mother's memories of the Great War. Like many in the East End she had been among the first civilians in the history of the world to suffer aerial bombardment. Those were the days of the Zeppelins, long airships that had begun the sad business of bombing civilians. She told me how one night, in the autumn of 1916, she heard shouting and screaming in the street and had gone outside. Above was a Zeppelin, a vast silvery cigar, lit up by crossed searchlights, its luminosity making it stand out brightly against the dark night sky. It was, Mother said, a frightening and menacing object. As she watched, it suddenly burst into flames.

An airship does not plunge to ground like an aeroplane but dies in slow motion, and there is time to savour the event. The crowd cheered, said my mother, and clapped. But above this commotion Mother remembered a woman crying out, 'What about the poor devils burning inside?' All over the East End people saw the Zeppelin's slow-burning descent which was visible for miles around. I suppose this was the greatest audience a dying aircraft, or dying men for that matter, has ever had. The Zeppelin crashed near Potters Bar. It had been shot down by one of the strange primitive aeroplanes of the day, a stringbag of wood, silk and piano wire. The pilot was Leefe Robinson, and he was awarded the VC.

After the Zeppelins came the Gothas in the summer of 1917. These were large German biplanes, the first aeroplanes to bomb London. Mother remembered them coming over by day, flying in a rigid diamond formation that was frightening in itself. There were no air-raid sirens in the First World War; instead, policemen cycled the streets blowing whistles. Nan found the Zeppelin and Gotha raids terrifying and even in the thirties she still talked about them, although these days they would be counted a mere nothing.

I stood with my companions as the headmaster read out the scholarship winners in sonorous tones: 'Phillips, Susman.' No surprise there, they had been thought certain winners. The headmaster paused. Would Hall, the disdainful, and Rosner, the bright-eyed, come next? But Hall was not as good as he thought he was and Rosner's brightness was but a pale moon to the blazing suns of Phillips and Susman. No, they had not made it, for

Zeppelins over the North Sea on their way to bomb London. This was the terrifying sight that my mother and her mother saw in the First World War. These airships were monsters of the night of a size that dwarfs even jumbo jets. *(IWM Q58450)*

results were given in alphabetical order. The headmaster paused again. Was that all? He cleared his throat and continued, 'and Wilson.' There was a gasp of surprise. That *was* all. Most people there had never thought of me as a prospect for I had always been well down in the list of school examinations. There were no other names, just the three of us: Phillips, Susman and me. I was linked with the great! I reflected that my error over the relative size of squares had not mattered.

The headmaster resumed. He said that he was always certain that Phillips and Susman would win the scholarship, but this was not the case with Wilson, for Wilson was erratic. But on that decisive day the adrenalin had flowed and, far from confusing my mind, had given it clarity and speed. I fancy that my unpredictability was connected with a lack of inner confidence that came from my background. Phillips and Susman came from an assured background, that of the middle class living comfortable lives, presumably unassailed by doubt. The headmaster allowed us winners to go home, there and then, to tell our mothers. I ran home as fast as my feet and my breath would allow.

Gone was my normal erratic progression from school to home. Gone was the slow shuffle, the minute inspection of every shop before passing on to the next one, all ignored as I raced home along Well Street, through Paradise Passage and along Darnley Road, panting with exertion and joy. I hurled myself down the stone steps of the airy of 12 Darnley Road and hammered on the door. My mother opened it. Fighting against my breathlessness, I panted to my mother, 'I've . . . won . . . the . . . scholarship!' We hugged each other. That day was one of the happiest days in all our lives. The first formidable barrier in life had been surmounted.

I met Ashley a few days later to tell him of my good fortune. 'I've won the scholarship,' I blurted out. 'How did you get on?' I expected him to match my success for he was a bright boy. It showed in the fine features of his face and in the quickness of his speech. But then I saw he was glum. He shook his head. Success had eluded him. But Buddy Matthews, who lived on the other side of Darnley Road, a languid boy who always came bottom of his class, had been successful. His headmaster thought it had been a mistake.

After my scholarship success came the slow enjoyment of selecting a school with mother and father. I had the choice of all the grammar schools in London, but the reputation of Merchant Taylor's and other famous schools counted for little to us in our ignorance. We looked only at the local schools and chose the foundation school of Parmiter's. It was a good school with a reputation for discipline. It still retains that reputation.

There was then another obstacle to surmount – the interview. Captain McArthur, the headmaster of Parmiter's, always interviewed prospective pupils whether they had won scholarships or not. Came the day and mother walked me from home down Mare Street to Bethnal Green. There, by the hospital, up a side street, we found ourselves standing in front of a formidable Victorian building, high and daunting. There we read from a large board: Parmiter's Foundation School. Mother led me through iron gates, across a grey tarmac court and through an arched entrance. A member of staff took us to the headmaster. A knock at the door and we were inside his study. The stern but kindly Captain McArthur waved us to a pair of chairs in front of the desk.

This was to be the first interview of my life, the first of many, but already I had been well versed in the art by Mr Verrier. I was with Mother when he gave his advice, what questions to expect and what answers to give. As we left he had said to Mother, 'Don't answer for him, Mrs Wilson, let the boy speak for himself.' The interview was successful and I was admitted to Parmiter's. The first of my ambitions had been secured. Or so I thought. But I had not reckoned on Adolf Hitler.

21   Munich

The Munich crisis came with the first falling leaves of September, ominous days which I still remember with dread. The air of an apocalypse hovered over us. There was fear; fear of bombing from the air and of poison gas creeping along the ground to choke us in our homes. Trenches were hastily dug in the park and sandbags were piled against buildings. The Underground closed and barrage balloons rose overhead. Gas masks were issued, swine-like death's heads, which transformed us into repulsive monsters. These were the grotesque harbingers of war. The thought of the holocaust to come was numbing. The world of the ideal home, the semi-detached house and the art deco lido faded before the sinister reality of trench, gas mask and gun. The dream had suddenly changed to nightmare, as dreams do.

Adolf Hitler had entered our lives and nothing would be the same again. All I knew of the crisis was that Herr Hitler, as Mr Chamberlain called him,

Equipping a refuge room. *(Reproduced with the kind permission of the copyright owner)*

WILLS'S CIGARETTES

EQUIPPING YOUR REFUGE ROOM — B

wanted to take bits of Czechoslovakia and would go to war to achieve this, and that our Prime Minster was flying to Germany to prevent it.

Everywhere there was much talk about gas, bombing and trenches. The trenches were horrible things. I saw them in the parks. They were long and narrow and zigzagged every few yards. They were dug just over 4 feet wide in order to seat two parallel rows of people. The open trenches were covered with concrete beams, making them elongated tombs that snaked across the parks. I imagined myself in one, closed in as if in a concrete communal coffin. I shuddered at the thought.

Gas was a particular horror and my mother's worst fear. The masks were horrible, clammy things smelling of rubber. 'Will they work?' asked mother, ever anxious. Sammy at school wondered how you could eat while wearing one. Why, you could starve to death if you had it on long enough. I reassured him. The chemicals in the gas mask would give out first so you would be gassed to death before you starved to death. He went quiet.

There was advice in periodicals normally devoted to the ideal home on how to make your rooms gas-proof. It made a change from the usual articles. A relative added to our fears when he pontificated that bombers could smother a city in a blanket of gas that would last for days. Our gas masks and gas-proof rooms would be exhausted by then. The fear of gas then was as great as the fear of nuclear war in the fifties and the praiseworthy actions of the government in the digging of trenches and issuing of gas masks did nothing to reassure us, but served to terrify and demoralise us into a state of panic.

The true meaning of war dawned on me. I had seen newsreels of what was happening in Spain's civil war but it had meant no more to me than a gangster film. War was something that happened to other people. Now it seemed that this unpleasant thing could happen to us. But it was not the fear of bombing alone that gave me a feeling of unknown dread. Nor was it the grotesque cartoons of war. It was simply the vague feeling that an unknown quantity had come on the scene; something that would change life in unknown ways. I knew that war was something to be avoided at all costs.

I asked my father about war, as I had once asked him about cricket. We talked and talked and somehow he conveyed to me its horror and its boredom. It was the boredom I feared most. I assumed that war was like measles, something you had to have and get over as soon and as quickly as possible. That it would be painful was certain, but how long would the pain last? I hoped it would be brief. So I asked, 'How long did the war last, Dad?' 'Four years.' I was dismayed. So long a time! And time goes so slowly when you are a child. How terrible that war could go on so long. Things would change and how I feared change. It was dreadful. Peace at any price became the philosophy of us all. The Prime Minister

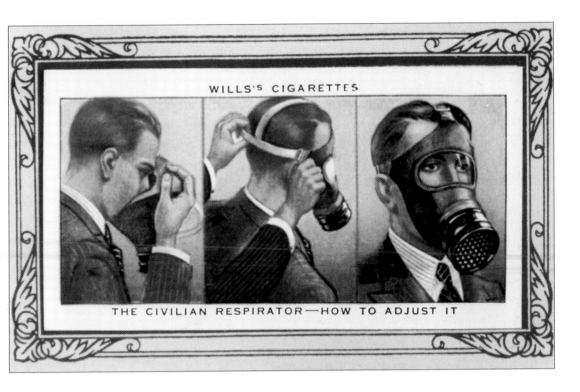

WILLS'S CIGARETTES

THE CIVILIAN RESPIRATOR—HOW TO ADJUST IT

Adjusting a gas mask. *(Reproduced with the kind permission of the copyright owner)*

summed up our feelings in a broadcast to the nation. 'How horrible, how fantastic, incredible it is that we should be digging trenches and trying on gas masks here because of a quarrel in a far-away country between people of whom we know nothing.' So much for Czechoslovakia! But we all agreed.

Munich remains etched in my memory in the shape of an old man in old-fashioned dress with an umbrella, waving a scrap of paper in the air. On the newsreels I saw the hysterical crowds cheering this man with the umbrella, smothering his car with their bodies, clinging for dear life to the bonnet, balancing on the running board, thumping the windows, thrusting hands inside to shake the hand of the man who had saved them. I saw him leaning out of an upper window at Downing Street waving that scrap of paper again. But his manner was too fanatically joyful and his face was lit with the disturbing light of a saviour. They said the Foreign Office had a ditty for Mr Chamberlain's aerial peregrinations between Croydon and Munich in his effort to appease Hitler. It ran:

'If at first you don't concede
Fly, fly, fly again.'

The crisis was soon forgotten. Everything went back to normal.

22 *Crystal Night*

It was Mr Williams who prepared me for the ten-plus scholarship but I was not a favourite. Once he caned me for no reason at all and, when I protested, said that it was for a future misdemeanour. Then there was the business of homework, which Mr Williams had given us as preparation for the ten-plus, and this I took seriously. Every time he examined my work, he stared at it in disbelief for it was always neat and tidy and good, so unlike my class work. He chided me in class, claiming that my work was not my own. In my report he wrote, 'His written work is very untidy and does not compare at all favourably with his work done at home.' He implied that I was cheating.

After I won the scholarship Mr Williams said doubtfully, 'I suppose I must congratulate you.' But he was not displeased. A scholarship won was a feather in his cap and he had taught me well. I moved up to the post-scholarship class of Mr Simmons, a fat lazy man, suitable for a class that lacked any incentive to learn. I relaxed in the afterglow of success and my school examination results grew worse and worse. I dropped well down the class list. When Mr Simmons read out the list and came to mine in fifteenth place he just shrugged his shoulders in resignation and said in puzzlement, 'I really don't know how you won the scholarship, Wilson.' But by then I didn't care.

One day in November, as I was walking along Darnley Road, Ashley beckoned me in. He was hot and bothered. He told me what Hitler and the Nazis had done to the Jews. Kristallnacht, Crystal Night, has a pretty sound of middle Europe in winter, but in 1938 it meant the night of broken glass, the night when, throughout Germany, Nazi thugs smashed the Jewish shops and set fire to them. I heard of it with despondency. Ashley said that he could not believe in Jesus Christ any more, despite our pact, as Hitler was a Christian. It had seemed a fair bargain but I had not reckoned with Hitler.

The film *Sixty Glorious Years* came as balm to our fear and wounded national pride. The world of Victoria admitted no doubts or hesitations. Her Britain had naturally assumed its pre-eminence among nations. There was none of that Munich kowtowing. The film was very popular and there were long queues waiting outside the cinema when mother took me to see it. It was full of exciting triumphs and I thoroughly enjoyed this heady nonsense.

More soothing was *Snow White and the Seven Dwarfs*, a sugary fantasy that served to calm the nerves of adult and child alike in that fearful autumn. Escapism was what we needed and was enjoyed in glorious Technicolor. Everything about this ultimate in Disney fantasy caught on. There was Snow White, too good to be true, and the wicked Queen who was too bad to be true. As I remember, the leader was Doc, assisted by Sneezy, Happy, Grumpy, Bashful, Dopey and Sleepy. I am not certain whether they were the seven deadly sins or the seven deadlier virtues but we boys took delight in insulting each other with one or other of the dwarfs' names. A plethora of kitsch appeared in the shops and I rather think it was the seven dwarfs that sparked the craze. I was able to supplement my museum with models of Snow White, her wishing well and the seven dwarfs. The ominous future was forgotten.

Christmas was approaching. At Orchard School there was feverish preparation for the festivities. We boys made Christmas decorations by pasting strips of coloured paper into linked rings. As the sticky chains grew, a mess of starch paste and crumpled paper piled on the floor. The teachers, atop stepladders, strung our handicrafts across the main hall.

On the final day of term lessons ended early and the class grew silent with suspense . . . waiting. Suddenly the classroom door was flung open and bakers, clad in long white overalls, entered, each man carrying a large tray of hot buns on his head. The sticky buns were the gift of a local Jewish baker whose son was in our class. We all set to and ate with gusto the large square buns, topped with sugar. Munich was forgotten and white snow came with Christmas Day.

23   *The Ides of March*

s 1939 dawned a feeling of unease prevailed. Around a sunlit pool of wishful thinking crept the dark weeds of a coming war. Only the newspaper astrologers and the *Daily Express* were optimistic. The new year edition of the *Daily Express* proclaimed, 'This is why you can sleep soundly in 1939. There will be no great war in Europe in 1939.' The message lacked conviction. The wail of the sirens practising alerts was contradiction enough and the trenches remained in Victoria Park, flooded now. Sandbags had rotted and split. We all knew in our hearts that 'Peace in our time' was a hollow promise.

The newsreels showed a beaten army and pitiful refugees crossing the Pyrenees. Refugees huddled in pathetic groups, filthy and bedraggled, clasping meagre bundles of possessions, the tattered remnants of their worldly goods. These were not the only refugees in the world that winter. There were Jews from Germany and Austria. At school the boys asked each other, 'Have you seen the refugees?'

But in all unfolding tragedies there is some light relief and in East London there was an absorbing diversion: boxing. Every Saturday night contests were held in the Devonshire Club in a street next to Darnley Road. Jack Solomons started his promotional career here. Now both have long passed into the limbo of history. These boxing promotions were very noisy events and much resented by those living in the neighbourhood, especially by the Hubbles and other superior people in Darnley Road. Crowds would gather outside the Devonshire Club and ascend in a solid mass iron stairs covered by corrugated vaulting. I often loitered at its entrance and gazed at the posters which advertised boxing bouts. These featured forthcoming attractions with large pictures of the fighters. That way I followed the rise of one Eric Boon, a protégé of Jack Solomon's.

Boon came from the country but he was adopted as a local hero. Then, unexpectedly, he became British champion when, behind on points, he knocked out the champion, Crossly. He was to become one of the participants in a famous boxing match. His opponent, Arthur Danahar, came from Bethnal Green, a true East Ender. Today the Boon–Danahar match is all but forgotten except by aficionados of the game. But in the dark days following Munich it became a national obsession. There was an

British boxers Eric Boon (left) and Arthur Danahar shaking hands at the weigh-in at the British Boxing Board of Control offices, before their lightweight title fight at Harringay Arena, London. Boon went on to win. Jack Solomons is on the left with his customary cigar. *(Hulton Archive)*

intense debate in the newspapers of the relative merits of the two contrasting pugilists. This debate was reflected in our schoolboy arguments. We divided into Boonites and Danaharites, as later we would divide into supporters of the Spitfire and the Hurricane.

On one side there was our adopted local hero, Eric Boon, squat and muscle-bound, undismayed when losing, whose dogged stamina and knockout punch time and time again snatched victory from the dark valley of defeat. By contrast, there was the elegant Arthur Danahar of Bethnal Green, a matchstick figure, thin and emaciated, with a classic boxing style. Boon and Danahar had one thing in common; they had defeated all their opponents in the ring. The newspapers took up the dispute with vigour and argued their merits at length. At last the matter was put to the test and they fought in February. It is sporting history that Eric Boon won an exciting fight, his dogged courage and never-say-die attitude giving him a classic victory. After a disastrous start and lagging behind on points, he won in the fourteenth round with a technical knockout – a last-minute victory. His resolute courage was a lesson to us all.

I remember as clearly as if it were yesterday that fateful day. It was 15 March 1939 – the Ides of March. In my mind's eye I can see a deserted Darnley Road. I can see a small boy, myself, walking down that road with not a car or a van or even a person in sight. Then I see a boy sitting on the sloping balustrade of the house next door to ours – Ashley. The scene remains carved in my mind, sharp and clear. I run up the stone steps and sit by him. 'The Germans have marched into Prague,' he says. I pretend to fall off the balustrade in sheer disbelief. 'You're joking. I don't believe you,' I say. And I did not believe him because I did not want to believe him.

Again and again I challenged him and again and again he denied that he was joking. At last Ashley convinced me and I reluctantly accepted the sickening truth. A chilling numbness crept over me – in a sense it has never left me – as the dread of coming war gnawed into my vitals. I knew in my heart of hearts, although I still refused to accept it in my mind, that war was inevitable. It hung over me as a recurring nightmare hangs over the would-be sleeper – with a sense of the dreaded coming of inevitable horror. I was just eleven and the world and my mind had become doom-laden.

On Good Friday, Mussolini invaded Albania – simple blatant aggression. The newsreels showed him haranguing the Italian crowds from a balcony with a bombastic performance. He was the image of the brute force that stood astride the world. I picked up the *Sunday Pictorial*. There blazoned across the front page was the headline, 'Why isn't Winston Churchill in the Cabinet?'

Later that month Chamberlain announced conscription. It affected me more than any of the other grim events of that spring and sent a chill through my heart. For suddenly the doings of the world impinged directly on my dreams. All men of eighteen were to be called up for six months (later it would be eighteen months) and I calculated that I would reach this age in seven years. My dream of entering university was under threat; I could well end up in the army instead. What a waste of time!

24　Parmiter's School

I left Orchard after the spring term and entered Parmiter's Foundation School. I said farewell to my best friend, Tony Stanley, whom I was never to see again, but otherwise I left Orchard without regrets, buoyed by fanciful expectations.

At Parmiter's my ambition was temporarily assuaged. I had started on my journey away from my working-class life with joy in my heart. While Father glowed with a vague pleasure at my going to a grammar school, Mother got down to the details. She told me of mysterious subjects that I would study: algebra, geometry and French. And she had heard that if I were good I would take Latin one day. This was the accepted measure of excellence in those days and I never questioned its wisdom.

Parmiter's, although its roots lay in Tudor times, was a Victorian school down to its last brick. I fell in love with its gaunt buildings that spoke a message of strict learning. The most persistent memory I have is of steel pen nibs, blackboards and desks of cast iron and heavy, scarred wood. A master, wrapped in a black gown, led us around the school. I remember vividly a certain blackboard and the chalking on it. The chalking intrigued me. I had seen words and numbers in boring abundance on the blackboards of Orchard, but these chalkings were different. They represented a complicated anatomical diagram, labelled with even more incomprehensible Latin names. I had no understanding of it, but to me it had the intriguing mystery of knowledge.

The day at Parmiter's started in the great hall with an assembly presided over by the headmaster, Captain McArthur. I was overwhelmed by the dark Victorian majesty of the hall, which impressed me far more than the light and airy modern hall at the Orchard. I felt I had moved into a new world. I noticed some boys standing outside at assembly. My neighbour told me they were the Jewish boys and since our morning assembly was a Christian service they did not attend. Later in the morning they would have an assembly of their own.

At Parmiter's I took to algebra with ease. However, there was one drawback to algebra, in the person of Fudge, the aged mathematics master. All the young boys at the school spread his dread reputation, so even before the first lesson I was in fear and trembling of this old man. Nor did he disappoint me in the flesh. There was absolute silence as, clad in a black gown, he strode into

the classroom and stood before us: a tall, gaunt man with white hair. He was every inch a stern Victorian. He believed in the Victorian ethic of doing things in the most difficult and laborious way possible.

Parmiter's School in the 1930s. *(LMA)*

His first words to the form were to forbid the use of fountain pens. He would not tolerate the fountain pen, with its soft gold nib; to him it was a horrid example of twentieth-century decadence. No, for him the instrument of writing was the Victorian nib of steel dipped into dark-blue Victorian ink of a peculiar consistency. The nibs and the grainy watery ink combined to make writing all but impossible. The flow of ink was irregular; either it held fast to the nib or would, unexpectedly, flood all too copiously on to the writing paper. Blots were dispensed with alarming alacrity and ink would not dry. The result – at least in my hands – was a sheet of spidery writing decorated with smudges. And woe betide the boy who broke a nib or threw a blot with these devices of an outworn technology. I cannot contemplate what Fudge, the upholder of Victorian values, would have thought of the modern ballpoint pen. Fudge was to us small boys a horrifying monster of a departed age, a dinosaur of schoolmasters. But I was told that he was kind and understanding to the older boys.

Although I could travel to Parmiter's by taking the bus to Bethnal Green Museum, I preferred to walk. It was a walk I loved, a solitary walk each day when I was lost in my own thoughts and feelings. It was a daily happy time, for I was still buoyed by the thought of going to grammar school. Moreover, I was now a boy of independent means, as I had been awarded a grant of £5 a term from the LCC. I had achieved my ambition, at least for the moment, and basked in the pleasure. My world seemed secure and my path in life certain. I had my friends at church and in Darnley Road, and was making new friends at Parmiter's, together with the pleasures of the extended family at Beale Place and Stevens Avenue. It would go on forever. It was just as well that I had this bliss and just as well that I could not see into the future.

My walk to Parmiter's took me down the long straight Framlington Park Road to Victoria Park, leaving the houses behind. I came to the Palm House, a graceful Victorian glasshouse – a miniature Crystal Palace. Often, when coming or going to school, I would stroll inside and admire the green tropical plants. This charming Palm House of cast iron exuded the calm certainty of a bygone era.

One day on my walk to school I saw a great silvery object wallowing on the ground not far from the Palm House, like a stranded manatee. I joined a small group of people watching a uniformed crew wrestling with this strange monster. What was it? 'It's a barrage balloon, son,' a small man told me. The barrage balloon was a sinister sign of the coming war. Or it should have been, but for some reason I did not see it that way. It did no more than excite my boyhood curiosity. During the coming weeks I would often join the crowd watching it. I hoped, as did the others, to see it inflated and rise up into the clouds. But we always waited in vain. It seemed the military, like the model powerboat hobbyists, played with their toys without getting anywhere.

As the summer weeks passed the balloon was joined by others, and by searchlights and guns. The peace of the park was disturbed. Little did I dream of the nightmare to come, when the joyful park would become a dismal armed camp and the green of the grass would give way to the grey of concrete gun emplacements and the brown of army huts; when bombs would destroy the Palm House. The park has since recovered, but a paradise lost is never quite regained. But this was the summer of 1939 and happily I would continue my journey, blissfully unaware of the horrors to come. At the edge of the park I would cross the Grand Union Canal and find myself at Parmiter's.

That summer we boys did not argue about Boon vs Danahar, Arsenal vs Spurs or Surrey vs Middlesex. No, that summer we found something different to dispute: Spitfires vs Hurricanes. These fighter planes had made their first public appearance and were yet to win fame and immortality in the Battle of Britain. Official opinion had once favoured the bomber, which would always get through, so they said. But something had changed. Certainly, we boys had eyes and ears only for these fighters. Did we possess some unconscious foresight that our futures would depend on them?

Their comparative merits were hotly debated, and as is the way of boys, this without any knowledge of their performance. Judging by the heat generated in these arguments, an eavesdropper might suppose that Spitfires were going to fight the Hurricanes and not the Messerschmitts. At first I favoured the Hurricane, I think because I liked the name. But one day I saw a photograph of the Spitfire against a blue, cloud-flecked sky. In its early version it had an elegance that has never been surpassed. I can see it now, that fastest of all aircraft of its day, seemingly floating immobile against the sky, a symbol of supreme calm and certainty. I became a convert. And as we know, in the end the Spitfire garnered the laurels of immortality because of its peerless elegance, while the Hurricane, unfairly, is almost forgotten. Strangely, in this era of Mach 3 aeroplanes – tubes of fire with stubs – the Hurricane and Spitfire are still remembered. They continue to appear as cutouts on the sides of cereal packets and still their performances are analysed in memoirs. These immortal twins of our liberty will be remembered when the Tornados, the F-16s and their ilk are long forgotten. Within a year the Hurricane and the Spitfire would go beyond schoolboy arguments and save the country in its hour of desperate need. Then it would no longer be Spitfire vs Hurricane, but Hurricane and Spitfire vs the Messerschmitt, the Heinkel, the Dornier and the Junkers.

A balloon barrage to protect London. I saw these being inflated in Victoria Park in the summer of 1939. *(IWC CH1518)*

25   Omens

By high summer of 1939 the omens of war had faded from my mind. The barrage balloons, trenches, guns and searchlights still remained in Victoria Park but their very familiarity bred complacency. At half-term I went to see my old headmaster at the Orchard. After a chat he gave me an errand to run. I was to deliver a piece of paper to another master. It was not in an envelope and as I walked down the corridor my prying nature got the better of me and I read it. The paper was an official minute. In it there were instructions on the evacuation of the school in war. A chill gripped my heart. Repressed fears returned and I felt sick with apprehension. Now there could be no doubt. War would come.

Omens do not come singly. On a June afternoon the *Thetis*, a brand-new submarine, sank in shallow waters on its first trial. It failed to surface after its one and only dive. A torpedo tube had been carelessly left open. It was found sunk, nose down, in shallow water, with its stern slanting above the waves at a grotesque angle. Newspaper photographs showed a disordered group of boats small and large gathered around the protruding stern. Rescue seemed near. Messages were tapped on the hull and those inside the submarine replied. Surely they could be saved! Yet the steel hull remained an impregnable barrier to the would-be rescuers.

The plight of the crew dominated everything. Our lessons at Parmiter's that Friday were interrupted as the masters gave the latest news. Mid-morning a delighted Fudge told us that two more men had escaped using the Davis escape chamber. We cheered at the news. It seemed that the rest of the crew would follow. But as the morning wore on no more news came. In the early afternoon the French master told us that something had gone wrong and, as the crew were running out of air, the rescuers were going to cut a hole in the protruding stern using an oxyacetylene torch. Disaster followed. An attempt was made to raise the *Thetis* higher in the water. Cables had been wrapped around her hull but during the attempt a swirl of waters had severed them. The *Thetis* rolled over, slipped beneath the waves and plunged 100 feet or so to the seabed. The final disaster. Rescue was impossible. The crew would slowly suffocate to death. I imagined them choking in the dark.

There was a common anger at the inefficiency. Why hadn't they tried to cut a hole in the hull sooner? Why was there no diving bell? Who was responsible for the carelessness that had lost the submarine? Why couldn't they save a submarine that was visible above the waves? The disaster was a further blow to our confidence in the nation. We all felt that the ghost of Ethelred the Unready was stalking the land.

At the end of June the Isle of Man Tourist Trophy (TT) came along. Tony Stanley, Jimmy Thomas and Lenny Fuller talked about their hero, the great British motorcyclist of the 1930s, Stanley Woods. He became my hero too. So it was that one day in June I sat by our Philco all-mains wireless set to listen to his triumph. Again, I had reckoned without Hitler.

The world of the TT had seemed far from the sinister world of Nazi Germany but it was not. Hitler had decided to invade the Isle of Man – with BMW motorcycles. They were to display the might of the Third Reich and we were to cower before them. Only the skills of the legendary Stanley Woods stood in their way. I desperately wanted him to win and followed the contest intently on the wireless.

Sadly, the race was not to be a triumphant ride for Stanley Woods. The competing BMWs were fitted with superchargers and won by brute force. The great Woods, with his superb skills, outmanoeuvred the BMWs on the twisty bends and moved ahead. I would breathe in relief for a moment only to hear with dismay the ominous growls of the BMWs as they let in their superchargers on the straights. Then, throbbing with menace, they roared past him. Their victory was inevitable. The deep undulating roar of their superchargers expressed perfectly the brutal might of Fascism and its philosophy. Stanley Woods did not stand a chance. A feeling of doom pervaded the commentary. There came across

WILLS'S CIGARETTES

AIR RAID WARDENS AND CIVILIAN VOLUNTEER DESPATCH-RIDER

Air-raid wardens, and a dispatch rider. *(Reproduced with the kind permission of the copyright owner)*

a feeling of helplessness in the face of an invincible force. I felt anguished at the defeat of Stanley Woods.

One summer evening Father came home complete with tin hat and gas mask. He had joined the air-raid precaution (ARP) and was cheerful. It came as a complete surprise to us, although it was a typical action on his part. My mother was hostile and worried. Hostile because he had not told her and because she saw this as yet another of his men's activities that took him away from home; and worried because she was a natural worrier who recognised the signs of coming war. With her curious brand of topsy-turvy logic she fatalistically confused cause and effect. I suspect that deep in her heart she saw gas masks, trenches and all the paraphernalia of air-raid precautions as the cause rather than the augury of impending war.

So Mother was angry with Father, implying that his action was helping to bring about a war. I am sure she felt that if she could persuade him to resign from the ARP then war would be prevented. She nagged at him incessantly. But her perverse logic did not prevail. The ARP was to become a second Men's Club to my father, and the warden's post a second clubhouse. During the war, when Darnley Road had gone, it was to become a second home. In a way he enjoyed the war, the thrill of danger and the companionship.

That summer the Anderson shelters came. They were issued free to those of the working class who had gardens or backyards. But they were only for the deserving poor. At 12 Darnley Road the Hubbles were too wealthy to qualify. I remember going around to Stevens Avenue to see the shelters arrive. The street was crowded, its inhabitants lining the pavements, waiting expectantly. At last a convoy of horse-drawn carts arrived, stacked high with the curved corrugated steel sections of the Anderson shelters. They were delivered in turn to each house in the street.

Father helped Grandpa and the Barts erect their Anderson in the small backyard of no. 17. Grandpa was old and Mr Bart from the flat downstairs was short and breathless, so all the hard work was left to my father. He had a knack for getting himself into these situations. He dug a large deep hole, for the Anderson shelter had to be half sunk in the ground. The operation was difficult because there was hardly space to put the excavated earth; the backyard was very small. After the hole was dug, my father and Mr Bart bolted the corrugated steel sections together. It was a strange object, a wrinkled steel thing without windows, half buried in the earth. Then, finally, father threw the dug earth on top of the shelter. The shelter all but filled the backyard, leaving but a narrow pathway between it and the garden fences. It stood there, a grey and sinister portent. We stood around and gazed at it, each one alone in his thoughts. There was no pleasure in the completion of the task. It was dusk and above us the summer sky was flushed with crimson.

26   Summer Camp

August came and the signs of impending war increased. More barrage balloons appeared in the skies and more guns and searchlights were placed in Victoria Park. Army huts arrived and men began painting kerbs white in preparation for the blackout. Hoods were fitted to traffic lights. The demoralising cries of sirens became more frequent – the despairing wail of a dying peace. At Nan's on Saturday afternoon the discussion was all about blackout, sirens and gas.

I felt that war was inevitable. Newspaper cartoons, more than mere words, conveyed to me the sinister aspect of coming war. No cartoonist was more skilful than Strube of the *Daily Express* at capturing this evil ambience in the baroque splendour of his cartoons, in which he engendered an atmosphere of the brutal armed might of Mars. His vivid drawings showed surly warriors arrayed in antique armour: ill-favoured Goliaths whose faces expressed the grossness of war. Grotesquely they rode not horses but modern caterpillar tanks.

Taking it easy on a lilo in front of my tent with Billy the Dog on a scouting holiday at New Romney in 1938. (*Author's collection*)

With fellow cubs and scouts of the St Luke's troop, Hackney, at New Romney in 1938. (*Author's collection*)

The time came for the annual scouts' camp and all thoughts of war were lost in the activities of preparation. Each year the Hackney cubs and scouts had a camp. In 1937 and 1938 it had been in New Romney, a place of marshes, sheep and humble churches of which St Mary's in the Marsh is the most famous. In 1939 it was to be at Hunstanton, a seaside resort on the north Norfolk coast. Money was short and I was disappointed to hear that we would not be going by train. Instead the whole camp, tents, equipment and people, were to be packed into the back of a lorry. It was a very old lorry, black and dilapidated.

When the day came priority was given to the packs of equipment and tents. Then we squeezed in among the bundles. The more regular-shaped ones served as seats for two or three ladies with us. We boys had to make do with the irregular packages and we pushed and shoved for these. As we trundled along I suppose we looked like something out of the *Grapes of Wrath*.

We travelled along the Lea Valley into the leafy suburbs of Epping, leaving the grey skies of London behind. It never entered my head as I was carried away from the grey streets that the ongoing cycle of my daily life would never be resumed. Never again would I go to the tuppenny rush at the Empress on Saturday morning or to Nan's on Saturday afternoon. Never again would I see 13 Beale Place. There would be no more walks in Victoria Park on Sunday mornings to watch the enthusiasts work their

With St Luke's Scout troop at Hunstanton in 1939. I am at the front with my hands on my knees. *(Author's collection)*

St Mary's in the
Marsh, New
Romney, 1938.
(Postcard)

model motor boats. No more Sunday lunches at Stevens Avenue and no more popping into Curtis's sweet shop on the way to Sunday school. I would never again see my treasured railway set. Fortunately, I was blissfully unaware of the disturbing future.

The flat landscape was not of great interest to us until we reached Ely. Then I marvelled at the Great Ouse that snaked its way through the countryside, its waters brimming the embankments that stood high above the flat fenlands. I had never seen such a strange landscape before. Eventually we arrived at Hunstanton by the sea.

That evening, after we had set up camp, we walked to the shore. It was a bright summer's evening and the setting sun glowed a benign red above the swell of the golden and black striations of a restless sea. We watched the waves break effortlessly against the broad sandy beaches.

27   War!

At the camp my father seemed to do everything, with Mr Browning, his minder, lurking quietly in the background. Father supervised the unloading of the lorry and organised the erection of the mess tent, which housed the camp's stores. He then set up the field kitchen. This was a home-made contrivance made out of a corrugated-iron drum and some used tin cans.

The following morning my father went to visit the local butcher to do a deal for the cheaper cuts of meat, such as scrag ends of beef and neck of lamb. The whole holiday was done on an incredibly low budget. My memory is vague, but was it really 1s 9d a week? That is about 10 new pence.

The spirit of do-it-yourself permeated the camp and each boy would make rustic racks out of twigs and sticks for the display of his utensils – mug, plate, knife, fork and spoon. We put our racks outside the flap of the tent each morning for daily kit inspection. In the evening my father would cook the meal in the field kitchen using the sticks we had gathered during 'wooding'. He was the cook as well as everything else and he prided himself on preparing an ample meal.

On the last night of camp we sat round a roaring log fire drinking cocoa, made without milk, singing campfire songs: 'There is a tavern in the town', 'She'll be coming round the mountain when she comes' and the like. We extemporised with many variations. Thus, 'She'll be wearing pink pyjamas when she comes.' The night darkened and the log fire roared up in flames, sparks flying in the air and then dying away. Soon there was nothing left but the bright glow of dying embers. We all drifted in a melancholic mood to our tents.

Next day the camp was broken up and the lorry loaded with our gear. Mother, Billy the dog and I were dropped off at the railway station: we were to extend our holiday in Northamptonshire and visit distant relations. Outside the railway station we saw off Father and the rest of the troop. We waved to them and they waved back as the lorry trundled off. I waved ever more frantically as the lorry shrank away. I waved them back to London and, although I did not know it, I was waving the friends of my young boyhood out of my life.

I was sad and lonely now that my friends had gone. Mother said I would soon get over it and I cheered up knowing I would see them again in two weeks' time. But it was not to be. Not then, not ever. I would never see any of them again. Nor would I ever to go to a scout camp again. The fissure in my life – war – was soon to come.

We caught our train and journeyed for hours through the maze of East Anglian railways. We took a car from a country railway station and found ourselves at a remote lodge in the Northamptonshire countryside.

A few days later, on 3 September 1939, in a crowded, small room of a neighbouring cottage, I heard the Prime Minister on the radio. He spoke in dreary monotonous tones without any emotion. 'This morning', he intoned, 'the British ambassador in Berlin handed the German government a final note stating that unless we heard from them by 11 o'clock that they were prepared at once to withdraw their troops from Poland, a state of war would exist between us. I have to tell you that no such undertaking has been received and that consequently this country is at war with Germany.'

These were passive and stilted phrases but they were chilling and received with dread. There was a silence as the company stared hollowly into space. Lives were going to be changed – we all knew that. There was some desultory conversation, but it was of mundane matters; nobody discussed the war and shortly afterwards the company broke up and departed for their Sunday lunches. Outside the cottage I burst into bitter and prophetic tears. I knew that things would never be the same again, and they never were.

I knew that a door had closed behind my life. I unconsciously sensed that I would never see my childhood friends, never see 12 Darnley Road again, and never see my toys and museum again. My sense of foreboding was justified. These things were now on the other side of that impenetrable door of time that was locked firmly against me. But it was a door made not of wood but of glass. Through it I could see the past, I can still see a past frozen in the aspic of time that we call memory. I can still see the actors performing their scenes again and again, scenes that never progress. The future was mere might-have-beens concealed behind opaque doors. Those doors will remain forever shut. I had wandered down another corridor and been propelled through a door to a future that I had never imagined. I felt a sense of loss and loneliness. Whatever the future held for me, the tree of my life had lost its connection with its roots. Later I would look back to the past wistfully; a poor but comfortable past, where families lived near each other and friends were in the next street. Now I sense that even before the war came I was jerking free from that old life. My ambition was not compatible with that life. Now I had entered a foreign world.

But my tears soon dried and my forebodings were forgotten. Life was pressing; it was harvest time, a strange and exciting time for a town child. It beckoned and I was taken out of myself. Outside the lodge, farm labourers had come up from the main farm at Stoke Doyle with tractors, reapers, horses and wains. I followed them to the harvest fields with Billy the dog.

Country life. On the farm, sitting on a hay tedder, near Oundle in Northamptonshire, 1939. *(Author's collection)*

Epilogue

I did not return to Hackney until 1946, a year after the war had ended. By then I had left grammar school and entered university – dreams fulfilled. But that's another story.

Hackney had changed much from the days of 1939. The war had wreaked its havoc. Large areas had been laid waste but St Luke's Church still stood proud among the ruins. No. 12 Darnley Road had been destroyed and so had my birthplace, 13 Beale Place in Bow. The shops of Frampton Park Road were no more. Victoria Park still bore the scars of war – it had been an armed camp crammed with anti-aircraft artillery and rockets – and drab army huts were still there. Its sports fields were given over to allotments for food, which was as scarce as it had been during the war.

Hackney after the war, with St Luke's in the background. (*Author's collection*)

Static water tanks were still to be seen, empty now of water but full of junk – old prams, mattresses. The gloom of the age of austerity was all-pervasive.

My friends from before the war had disappeared, moving away to the suburbs and beyond during the turmoil of war and its aftermath. The congregation of St Luke's Church was made up of strangers. There was no return to the thirties. The severance from my childhood life was complete. In 1951 I married and moved away from Hackney.

The wasteland that was Hackney after the war. *(Author's collection)*